WATER

&

BLOOD

An Account Of The Life Of The Messiah

Phil Hinsley

authorHOUSE®

AuthorHouse™ UK
1663 Liberty Drive
Bloomington, IN 47403 USA
www.authorhouse.co.uk
Phone: 0800.197.4150

Published by AuthorHouse 09/26/2014

ISBN: 978-1-4969-9091-4 (sc)
ISBN: 978-1-4969-9092-1 (e)

In grateful thanks to Jack and Pat

Also by Phil Hinsley

*The Dragon the World and the Christian
Strangers*

Bibliography

Aharoni & Avi-Yonah. *The Macmillan Bible Atlas.* (1997)

Barclay, William. *Jesus as they saw him* (SCM Press Ltd. 1991)

, *The Plain Man Looks At The Apostles' Creed* (Fontana Books. 1972)

Bock, Darrell. L. *Luke* (IVP. 1994)

Bruce, F.F. *The Gospel of John* (Eerdmans Publishing Company. 1994)

Clanchy, M.T. *Abelard A Medieval Life* (Blackwell Publishers. 1999)

Cole, R. Alan. *Mark* (IVP. 1989)

Cruden, A. *Complete Concordance to the Old and New Testaments* (Lutterworth. 1969)

Davidson, Ivor. J. *A Public Faith* (Monarch Books. 2005)

France, R.T. *Matthew* (IVP. 1985)

Green, Michael. *The Message of Matthew* (IVP. 2000)

Lutterworth Dictionary of the Bible (Lutterworth Press. 1994)

Morris, Leon. *The Gospel according to John* (Eerdmans. 1995)

Tasker, R.V.G. *John* (IVP. 1974)

Taylor, Barbara. *The last Asylum* (Hamish Hamilton. 2014)

Wright, David. F. *Heretics* (Houghton Mifflin Harcourt. 2011)

Wright, Johnathan. *Councils and Creeds* (A Lion Handbook. The History of Christianity. 1990)

Philip found Nathanael and told him, "We've found the one Moses wrote about and about whom the prophets also wrote – Jesus of Nazareth, the son of Joseph."

"Nazareth! Can anything good come from there?"

"Come and see."

John the apostle

Introduction

When a friend heard that I was writing a book on Jesus, he exclaimed, "Why write another book on Jesus?" That is a good question. Why should I add to the mountain of books that are already available to anyone who is interested? My motivation in writing this account of the life and teaching of the one that millions call Lord and Saviour is the concern that to a great extent the teaching of Jesus is not as well known as most people assume.

Most of us rely on what others have told us or what we have seen in films concerning this unique life and have not read his recorded words for ourselves. For those who have read for themselves the biblical accounts their response to what they have read is often coloured and shaped by their own denominational position which can vary greatly from one fellowship to another. What did he really say about heaven and hell? Why is he returning to earth? What is the reward of the saved and what future does this planet have? Perhaps the greatest question is: What is the destiny of man, and what has Jesus to do with it?

Some of the things Jesus said shocked those he spoke to and many of his followers left him. The response of others came in aggressive rejection, confused bewilderment and scepticism. For others he had the words of eternal life. It is the same today.

This is as good a time as any to take the invitation of an introduction to the Jesus of the Bible. We live in a world of conflicting voices telling us what is true while disagreeing with those who claim to promote the same name. I do not speak on behalf of any group or fellowship, neither am I a member of any group or sect. Listen to him – it may change your life.

For this account I have used, adapted and paraphrased, the New International Version © 1973, 1978, 1984 by the International Bible Society.

Contents

Bibliography...vii

Introduction...xi

Contents xiii

Prologue..xv

The stranger 1

Contact with the Messiah...7

Facing the enemy 9

John and the Messiah 14

Food from the Messiah...20

The Messiah's real food and drink......................................23

The family of the Messiah 26

Jews and Gentiles 28

Only two groups 36

The shut door 45

The religious establishment...49

Dining with a Pharisee 62

Collusion with the devil 65

The Messiah and anxiety 68

The Messiah and deception 74

Talking to God Part 1 86

Your will be done on earth Part 2.......................................88

Our daily needs Part 3 92

Forgiveness Part 4...94

Temptation and the evil one Part 5.....................................98

The Reward...102

The Messiah and his Father 111

The Messiah and blindness 125

The Messiah and the human heart 134

The Messiah and the resurrection 142

The Messiah and judgment 150

The Messiah and healing 158

The Messiah's identity 169

The Winter Feast 173

Why the Messiah had to die 175

The Messiah's time has come 180

The Messiah's last Passover 183

Arrest and trial 187

The Messiah crucified 195

The Messiah rises 202

The Messiah's Spirit 208

Last thoughts 216

About the Author 221

Prologue

She had decided to be strong. No outstretched arms and wailing as she had seen other mothers do at funerals, yet some emotions could not be controlled. Her lower lip trembled, her throat tightened and her breathing was laboured. She turned and with gratitude saw that most of the village had come together in this time of grief to support her as her only son was buried.

Her husband had died a few years earlier causing her to rely on their son for their income. He was almost eighteen when he had been taken ill; although the local doctor did his best for him he was not able to stem the deterioration that held the young man in its deadly grip. Within six days he was dead.

That was yesterday and now they were walking through the village gate. She tried to hold down her rising emotions as her eyes moistened and tears began to run down cheeks. She blinked her tears back and swallowed. Just in front of her the stretcher bearing her son was being carried to the burial ground.

Her attention was drawn to the rising dust as a large group of travellers, including women, who were approaching the village from the north road which led to the densely populated province of northern Galilee. All of them were carrying supplies over their shoulders and as the two groups came together the travellers paused to allow the funeral procession to continue on their way. One of the men at the front of the group who had a wineskin and bedroll over his shoulder took them off and handed them to his companion and moved towards to stretcher.

He was a short stocky man dressed in the worn leathers that identified him as someone used to working in the stone quarries and timber yards. His dark curly hair was cut short and his beard was full and covered much of his cheeks down to the front of his neck. His face carried the flinty look of a man who had experienced many difficulties.

As he looked towards the body on the stretcher he appeared to be moved by what was happening. He turned to the mother and said, "Don't cry," and perhaps because of his concerned expression she allowed him to walk the few steps to where the stretcher was being held steady by the four bearers. The body was covered except for the face. He then put his hand onto the body which caused the bearers to tighten their grip on the two poles as it was against traditional custom to touch a dead body. By now the strangers and the villagers had crowded around the stretcher wondering what this man's intention was. The mother stared at the man and was about to tell him that he should move on when she heard him speak to her dead son.

"Young man, listen to me; get up!" This was enough to provoke the mother to move towards the man and she went to grab his arm when everyone went silent. All that could be heard was a sharp intake of air as her son sat up and rubbed his eyes with the sheet that still covered most of his body. He managed to mumble some words as the stranger broke into a broad smile that changed his normally austere expression and he helped him off his stretcher as the shocked bearers quickly lowered it to the ground and stood back. With his arm around the quivering young man's shoulders he placed him into the outstretched arms of his mother who was now openly crying with joy and astonishment.

An event like this had never been seen before; they had only heard tales of long ago in the lives of their most famous prophets where the dead were raised but those accounts were considered more as legends than historical facts. They saw it with their own eyes and fear filled them as they absorbed the greatness of what happened. "He must be a great prophet that God had sent to help his people in their time of need just like the ones we've been taught about from the law," they said.

"What's his name?" They excitedly asked as he rejoined his group and slung the wineskin and bedroll back over his shoulder and lifted his leather hood over his head as a shield from the sun.

"Jesus," they told them, "we've come from Capernaum."

The news of this event spread like wildfire throughout Galilee.

The stranger

Tiberius Claudius Nero, stepson of Augustus, and Caesar of the Roman Empire was in the fifteenth year of his reign. Pontius Pilate[1] was governor of Judea. Herod Antipas, son of Herod the Great was ruler of Galilee, his brother Philip ruler of Iturea and Traconitis which was north-east of the Sea of Galilee, and the third brother Lysanias ruled in Abilene, which was north of the other areas that his brothers ruled over. The high priest was Caiaphas and the previous high priest was Annas but he was deposed by the Roman governor Valerius Gratus, prefect of Judea in AD 15. Five of his sons and one grandson became high priests. Caiaphas was his son-in-law, yet Annas remained active behind the scenes.

The weathered and tanned man was clothed like a famous prophet who had lived over 800 years before. He stood still, waist deep in the cold fast moving water of the river. He had done this hundreds of times before on colder days but this day was bathed in sunshine and it seemed that all the people from the city and the villages were coming to him.

A growing line of people began making their way down into the river towards him. He faced the first who was an elderly woman. He gripped her bony shoulders with his strong hands and lowered her down until her head was submerged below the water. It may have

---

[1] He gained the appointment as Prefect of Judea in AD26 (his correct title was discovered in 1961 on an inscription in Caesarea).

seemed longer than it was but when he lifted her almost clear of the water she was smiling broadly and then made her way shivering back to the bank side where friends covered her with a large towel.

His message was a stark warning: God's anger is coming soon and the only way to escape that fiery judgment was to stop rebelling against him and submit to a ritual that was reserved for the unclean gentiles who wanted to join themselves to Israel which amounted to a complete washing. This would symbolise being cleansed from their sin and acceptable before God. Gentiles were considered as unfit to worship God unless they were submerged in water and all male Gentile converts had to be circumcised.

Some of the Jews would not undergo this demeaning ritual of washing as they believed themselves already close to God because of their heritage as children of Abraham but this man of the desert told them that their racial stock made no difference to God and that all needed to repent. This deeply upset and angered the religious leaders who considered themselves better than the common person and closer to God because of the many rules and rituals they diligently followed.

This outsider should have been named Zechariah, like his father, and worked his allotted time each year in the temple as a descendent of Aaron, from the priestly tribe of Levi. Thirty years previously, while his father performed his duties as a priest in the temple an angel appeared to him and he froze with fear. For a long time he and his wife had not been able to have a child of their own and they were both getting older. The angel spoke to him, "Don't be afraid Zechariah, your prayer has been heard and your wife Elizabeth will have a son and you'll name him John. He will be a great joy to you and many will be happy because of his birth. He will be great in God's eyes but he's never to drink wine or any other fermented drink. From his birth he'll be filled with the mind of God – his Holy Spirit.

"Because of what he'll do many will return to God, and he'll be like Elijah, turning the hearts of parents to their children and the disobedient to a better way. In doing this he will be preparing the people for God's arrival."

But Zechariah had doubts, "How can I be sure of this? My wife and I are old."

"I am Gabriel[2]. I stand in the presence of God and I've been sent to you with this good news, but because of your doubt you'll not be able to speak until the day you name him."

When that day came, eight days after he was born, the neighbours and relatives were expecting the baby to be named after the father but Elizabeth told them, "No! He's going to be called John."

"There's no one among your relatives with that name," they answered. They appealed in signs to his father what name he wanted for the child and he asked for something to write on and he wrote, "His name is John." From that moment on he was able to speak again and his neighbours were amazed and the news of what happened spread quickly over the whole area. Everyone who heard about it wondered what this special child would grow up to become.

John grew up to be independent and strong minded. He lived in the desert until the right time came to fulfil his commission.

Those who came to John acknowledging their sins were baptized[3] but those who came with a hardened heart, as the religious leaders did, were bluntly told that they were a brood of snakes that needed to listen to the warning that God's wrath was coming. They also needed to produce the evidence that they were repentant and not just putting

---

[2]   *Gabriel* means 'man of God'

[3]   *Baptise* means 'to immerse' but also points to a change having taken place.

on an act so that they looked pious. "Every tree," John told them, "that doesn't produce fruit will be cut down and thrown into the fire and the axe is already at the root of the trees."

"Are you the Anointed One – the Messiah?"

"I'm definitely not." He shot back.

"Who are you then?" they asked him, "Are you Elijah?"

"I'm not" he answered.

"Are you the Prophet?"[4]

"No."

"We need to take an answer back to those who sent us, so tell us, who do you say you are?"

John answered, quoting words written down many centuries earlier, "I am the voice of one calling in the desert, preparing the way for the Lord, making straight in the wilderness a highway for our God. Every valley will be raised up and every mountain and hill made low; the rough ground will become level, the rugged places a plain. And the glory of the Lord will be revealed, and all mankind together will see it."

"So why do you baptize if you're not the Messiah, nor Elijah, nor the Prophet?"

"I baptize with water, but there's someone among you that you don't know who will baptize you with the Holy Spirit[5]and with fire. He is the one I'm preparing for, the thongs of whose sandals I'm not

---

4   See Deut. 18:15-19

5   God's mind and nature

worthy to untie. He holds his winnowing fork to clear his threshing-floor and to gather the wheat into his barn, and he'll burn up the chaff with unquenchable fire."

The last prophet in the Old Testament, Malachi, had written, "Surely the day is coming; it will burn like a furnace. All the arrogant and every evildoer will be stubble, and that day that is coming will set them on fire," says the Lord Almighty. "Not a root or a branch will be left to them. But for you, who revere my name, the sun of righteousness will rise with healing in its wings and you will go out and leap like calves released from the stall. Then you'll trample down the wicked and they'll be ashes under the soles of your feet on the day when I do these things," says the Lord Almighty.

"Remember the law of my servant Moses, the decrees and laws I gave him at Horeb for all Israel.

"See, I'll send you the prophet Elijah before that great and dreadful day of the Lord comes. He'll turn the hearts of the fathers to their children, and the hearts of the children to their fathers; or else I'll come and strike the land with a curse."

John knew the Messiah was coming but he did not know exactly what would happen then or what the Messiah would do first; all he knew was that from that time on everything would change – for the glory of Israel and for judgment on the world.

He was preaching a baptism of repentance for the forgiveness of sins[6] and many were coming to him acknowledging that they had trespassed and fallen short of the standard given in the law and through the prophets. A number of them wanted to be his disciples yet he did not know how to recognise the Messiah when he would eventually see him. What would he look like? Could he tell who he

---

[6]   1 John 3:4

was by just how he looked or what clothes he wore? How would he know?

Isaiah had written, 'He had no beauty or majesty to attract us to him, nothing in his appearance that we should desire him.'[7]

God had sent John and he would provide the identification that John needed, and it would be a unique sign that would set the Messiah apart from everyone else who would be there at that time. This is what John was to look out for – a dove would land on the Messiah and remain on him – an unnatural event, as this would be, was the sign by which John could identify the Messiah.[8]

From then on John scanned the crowds for any man with a dove on his shoulder.

---

[7]   Isa 53:2b

[8]   John 1:32-34

Contact with the Messiah

John's mind was drawn to visualising what would happen when he finally comes face to face with the Messiah. His thoughts ranged over the many places in Scripture that spoke of his coming[9] and wondered when and how the Messiah's reign would begin.

On that hot day in the arid land surrounding the River Jordan east of Jericho John saw him among those lining up for baptism. His eyes were fixed on this unremarkably looking man who was shorter than most men and looked like he was used to hard manual work. He stood in line looking at John and was wearing a brown linen tunic and calf length trousers. Over his arm he carried a much used knee-length leather jerkin and a wide work belt that held various leather pouches that had at one time contained his tools. This was not a man with the bearing of the long awaited Messiah, his only distinguishing feature was his unattractiveness as a man, yet the unmistakable sign was there. There was a dove on his shoulder. The others waiting for their baptism saw John's attention and gave way to the man with the bird on his shoulder. What was to happen next would shock and puzzle John because in all his thinking of what the Messiah would do he never imagined what the next few moments held.

The stranger with a dove resting near the side of his face now stood waist high in the flowing water waiting for John to baptize him.

---

[9]   Isa 9:7, 13:9, 30:23, Mic 4:3, Zep 2:2, Zec 14:9, Mal 3:2.

"I can't baptize you", John spluttered, "I'm the one who needs to be baptised by you, not you by me!"

"You know who I am but it's important for me, an Israelite, to go through this ritual because of what is planned for me."

Then John, without fully understanding the need for this holy and righteous person to be baptised, submitted to his request and immersed him into the cold water. The dove flapped its wings and hovered over the water as the whole body of this man was plunged below the surface. As he came out of the water the dove returned to him and suddenly the sound of a voice was heard from above, "This is my Son, whom I love and I am delighted with him."

The Messiah's name was Jesus.[10] John would not see him again for the next six weeks.

---

[10]   The name means 'Yahweh saves' Mic 5:2. 'Joshua' in Hebrew.

Facing the enemy

Jesus knew he had to face the unseen ruler of the world who through his lies had deceived all who lived on the earth.

Later he was to say to his critics, "You belong to your father, the devil, and you want to carry out your father's desire." Jesus was confronted by those who were violently opposed to him, and he went on to say, "He was a murderer from the beginning, he didn't remain with what is true because there's no truth in him. His native language is lying – he's a liar and the father of lies," In directly facing his enemies Jesus told them that the person who belongs to God hears what God says and the reason they would not listen to him was because they did not belong to God.

The Apostle Paul was later to write, 'Satan himself masquerades as an angel of light.'[11] Long before the creation of humans, billions of years ago, Satan was here on earth but then he was known as the 'Morning star, son of the dawn – the shining one – Lucifer.'[12] He was blameless from the day he was created till wickedness was found in him. He had been the model of perfection, full of wisdom and perfect in beauty. He had been in Eden, the garden of God. He was an angel of the highest order until pride corrupted him.[13] Jesus told his

---

[11]   2 Cor 11:14

[12]   Isa 14:12

[13]   Ezek 28:12-17

disciples that he saw Satan fall like lightning from heaven.[14]Satan had attempted to overthrow God and in that rebellion the planets in our solar system were destroyed. The devastating effects of that angelic war is seen in the mass of craters on our moon and on other planets, and even on earth, caused by the heavy bombardment that occurred in this part of the galaxy, if not in other parts as well. When Noah and his family left the ark he was told to replenish the earth, just as the first humans were commanded to do. How long this earth remained in its chaotic and desolate state is not known, but in the darkness of that age Satan remained here, waiting.

From being identified as an Israelite and going through the ritual of baptism by which he set the pattern for his followers; that is to do what Adam and his descendents had failed to do, Jesus entered the desert, the habitation of wild animals. He was there for forty days and was without food and so his physical condition became desperately weak. This forty day period was to recreate on an individual level the forty years of testing that the Israelites went through. The Israelites, except for a few significant exceptions, remained in a continuous state of rebellion against God, and now a descendant of the tribe of Judah was to be tested to the limit as to whether he would give in under extreme pressure or remain obedient even though he was to come close to death and be tempted to ease his painful difficulties by the ruler of this world.

Knowing how hungry Jesus was, Satan suggested that if he really were the Son of God why doesn't he command those rocks close to his feet to become freshly baked bread?

The heat during the day and the cold of night made their thirst and discomfort even harder to bear and complaining about the leadership came naturally. The Israelites were to live and die (except for two individuals who were adults when they left Egypt) in complaint

---

[14]   Luke 10: 18

and anger at the difficulties they had to experience and against God himself for putting them and their families through such an ordeal.

At the end of those forty years when the Israelites wandered in the desert Moses wrote for those who were now about to enter the Promised Land, "Remember how the Lord your God led you all the way in the desert these forty years, to humble and test you in order to know what is in your heart, whether you would keep his commandments or not. He humbled you by causing you to hunger and then feeding you with manna, which you or your parents had not known of before, to teach you that man does not live by bread alone but by every word that comes from the mouth of the Lord.

"Your clothes didn't wear out and your feet didn't swell during those forty years. You need to understand that as a parent disciplines his son, so the Lord your God disciplines you."[15]

The forty years was for each of the forty days that twelve Israelites (one from each tribe) explored the land and that ten of them brought back a disheartening report that exaggerated the difficulties ahead of them, but two of them, Caleb, from the tribe of Judah and Joshua, from the tribe of Ephraim, were confident of taking over the land. Tragically the majority negative view set the people into a major grumbling session where they wanted a change of leadership and a return to Egypt. As a result of this critical attitude all those over twenty years old, except for Caleb and Joshua, would die in the desert and their children, who they complained would die there, would in fact be the ones to enter the land.

Jesus was suffering with the effects of his forty days in the wilderness. The Israelites had repeatedly failed and became angry with God because of the way they were being led by Moses and by God himself. Jesus was intimately aware of what happened to the tribes of Israel in the wilderness and was determined not to repeat their rebellion. In answer to the suggestion from Satan of creating

---

[15]   Deut 8: 2-5

11

bread to keep himself alive, Jesus knew that doing it would have meant denying his character of obedience to his Father.

"It is written," Jesus responded, "Man does not live on bread alone, but on every word that comes from the mouth of God."

Satan distorts and misapplies Scripture and his next temptation was to use a section of one of the psalms to imply that the Messiah, or any servant of God, would experience no personal injury because the angels are charged with protecting him, but to foolishly and deliberately put yourself in danger and then bank on God rescuing you is to manipulate the Scripture and put God to the test.

Jesus felt gusts of cold wind buffeting his body and looking down he realised that he was standing close to the edge on the highest tower of the temple in Jerusalem. His eyes took in the 450 feet to the rocky bottom of the Kidron Valley below, and Satan said, "Jump! You'll be safe – God has given his promise of protection."

The whole Israelite community, numbering perhaps three million people, set out travelling from one location to the next and very soon there came a water shortage. The people complained to Moses, "Give us water to drink!"

"Why quarrel with me?" Moses replied, "Why are you putting the Lord to this test?"

The thirst was real and the complaints intensified. "Why did you bring us up out of Egypt? Was it to make our families and livestock die of thirst?"

"What am I to do with these people?" Moses asked God with anger and frustration, "They're close to stoning me!"

"Walk ahead of the people," God told him, "and take some of the leaders of Israel with you. Take the staff you struck the Nile with and

I'll stand before you at the rock at Horeb. Hit the rock, and water will come out of it for the people to drink. Moses did as he was instructed and enough water came flooding out for everyone's needs.

Moses called that place Massah and Meribah[16] because the Israelites quarrelled and tested the Lord saying, "Is the Lord among us or not?"

Much later Moses wrote, "Do not test the Lord your God as you did at Massah."[17]

Again Jesus quoted Moses, "Do not put the Lord your God to the test." From being on the edge of a precipice he suddenly found himself on another high place but without any danger of falling. He somehow could see all the kingdoms of the world and all their splendour and that darkly familiar voice spoke into his ear, "I'll give you all their authority and greatness because they're mine to give so I can give it to anyone I choose. All you have to do is acknowledge me as your Lord and they're all yours to do with as you wish – what do you say?"

Moses, knowing that the Israelites were to enter a land full of deities, warned them to "Fear the Lord your God; serve him only and take your oaths in his name. Do not follow other gods that you will soon find out about because the Lord your God, who is among you, is a jealous God and his anger will burn against you and he will destroy you from the face of the land."

Jesus quickly turned to the voice and said, "Leave me Satan! It's written, 'Worship the Lord your God, and serve only him.'[18]

The adversary of God then left Jesus close to death and immediately angels were by his side giving him the physical help he needed.

---

[16]   *Massah* means *testing* and *Meribah* means *quarrelling*

[17]   Deut 6:16

[18]   Deut 6:13

John and the Messiah

John looked up from what he was doing and saw Jesus walking towards him. "Look," John excitedly said to his disciples, "The Lamb of God, who takes away the sin of the world!" He explained to them how he was not able to identify the Messiah until God revealed to him how he could identify him and John finished what he was saying with the momentous words, "I've seen him and I can truly say that he is the Son of God."

The next day John was talking to two of his disciples when he saw Jesus walking past. "There he is!" John said to them, and they left John and began following Jesus. When Jesus became aware of what they were doing he stopped and turned to them and asked, "What do you want?"

"Rabbi," they said, "where are you staying?"

"Come and I'll show you."

They went back to where he was staying and spent that day with him. Later, Andrew, one of the two who went to where Jesus was staying, left to find his brother Simon and he told him, "We've found the Messiah!" And he took him to meet Jesus.

Looking at Simon, Jesus said, "Your name is Simon son of John, you're also going to be known as Peter.[19] The next day Jesus decided to move to Galilee where he found Philip, who like the other disciples came from Bethsaida which was on the north east coast of the Sea of Galilee, and said to him, "Follow me."

Philip quickly found Nathanael, who was from Cana, about eight miles north of Nazareth, and said to him, "We've found the one Moses wrote about and the prophets also – Jesus of Nazareth."

"Not Nazareth! Can anything good come out of that city?" Nathanael sniggered.

"Then come and see for yourself," Philip replied.

"Here's a true Israelite," Jesus said to Nathanael, "without any deceit."

"Do you know me?" he asked.

"Before Philip called you I saw you under the fig-tree." Something about that statement caused Nathanael to exclaim, "Rabbi, you're the Son of God – the King of Israel."

"Because I saw you under the fig-tree you believe," a surprised Jesus said, "You'll see greater things than that. I'm telling you the truth; you'll see heaven opened and angels of God moving between me and heaven."

Very soon afterwards a wedding took place in Cana. Jesus and his disciples were invited as well as his mother and his four brothers and two sisters. During the banquet it was discovered that the wine had run out. Mary informed Jesus of this embarrassing event. He spoke quietly and respectfully to his mother, "Woman, my time has

---

[19]   Or Cephas in Aramaic, the language they spoke in.

not yet come and my concerns are not yours." Mary nevertheless told the servants to do whatever Jesus told them. He said to them, "Fill those large jars with water." The stone jars were the kind used for ceremonial washing, each of them could hold many litres of water. They filled them to the brim and he told them to draw some out and take it to the man who had responsibility for the wedding. When the master of the banquet tasted the water that had been changed into wine he called the bridegroom aside and said, "It's the usual practice on occasions like this to bring out the best wine first and when the guests have had plenty to drink then the inferior wine comes out but you've saved the best till now."

After this he went down to Capernaum with his family and his disciples and they stayed there for a few days.

A disagreement arose between some of John's disciples and a person who had some issues concerning ceremonial washing and then John was told that the disciples of Jesus were baptising and everyone was going to him.

John knew his position and said in answer to them, "A man can only receive what is given him from above. Remember what I said, I'm not the Messiah; my work was to prepare a people for his coming. The bride belongs to the bridegroom. The best-man waits and listens for him, and is overjoyed when he hears his voice. That joy is mine, and it's now complete. He must become greater; I must become less."

Shortly after saying this John was arrested and imprisoned in the fortress Machaerus, east of the Dead Sea. This was because John was critical of Herod who had married Herodias, his brother's wife, plus all the other corrupt things he had done.

John's disciples were still able to keep him informed about the growing interest in the reported miracles being done by Jesus yet because of the many prophesies relating to the coming of the Messiah,

John was becoming concerned that what he believed would happen, hadn't happened.

John sent two of his disciples to Jesus to ask him if he was the one who was to come, or should we expect someone else? With the great expectation shared by many of the imminent arrival of the Messiah and the liberation that Israel would experience with the removal of the Romans and Israel's promotion to the head nation in the world there arose a degree of impatience and puzzlement over the ministry of Jesus which concerned John and many others.

This important question was put directly to Jesus by the two sent from John. At that same time Jesus cured many who had diseases, sicknesses and evil spirits, and he gave sight to many who were blind. Jesus answered John's messengers by saying, "Go back and report to John what you've seen and heard: The blind receive sight, the lame walk, those who have leprosy are cured, the deaf hear, the dead are raised, and the good news is preached to the poor. Blessed is the man who doesn't fall away on account of me."

Jesus did not solve the injustices and wickedness of his time, anymore than he does now, and this has led many to dismiss and reject him as the Messiah. Jesus always pointed to the kingdom of God and its establishment at his return as bringing the solution to all the world's evils. Until then this world is under the control of the evil one[20]and his servants will have to live in what is enemy held territory. That is why years later Paul wrote, 'Finally, be strong in the Lord and in his mighty power. Put on the full armour of God so that you can take your stand against the devil's schemes, because our struggle isn't against humans, but against evil spiritual rulers and powers in this dark world.'[21]

---

[20]   1 John 5:19b

[21]   Eph 6:10-12

After they left Jesus spoke to the crowd about John: "What did you go out into the desert to see? A reed swaying in the wind or a man dressed in fine clothes? Of course not, those who wear expensive clothes and live in luxury are found in palaces. John is the one about whom it's written: 'I will send my messenger ahead of you, who will prepare your way before you.'[22] I'm telling you; of those that are born there is no-one greater than John; yet the one that's least in the kingdom of God is greater that he is." The life of those who inherit the kingdom of God will be everlasting and sinless.

"So to what can I compare this generation? They're like children sitting in the market-place calling to each other, 'We played the flute for you, and you didn't dance; we sang a mournful song and you didn't cry.'

"For John the Baptist came neither eating nor drinking the same things most people eat and drink, and you say, 'he has a demon.' The Son of Man[23]came eating and drinking the same things you eat and drink and you say, 'here's a glutton and a drunkard, a friend of tax collectors and "sinners".' But God does his work through different people in different ways."

Herod's wife, Herodias, nursed a grudge against John and wanted to kill him but Herod feared John and protected him, knowing him to be a righteous and holy man. Herod listened to John with a mixture of feelings; from fear to puzzlement, but he enjoyed listening to him.

On Herod's birthday he gave a banquet for his high officials, military commanders and leading men of Galilee. When Salome[24]the daughter of Herodias came in and danced, everyone was pleased, especially Herod who had fantasised over her for some time. He

---

[22]   Mal 3:1

[23]   Dan 7:13

[24]   Salome was married to her uncle at the time.

foolishly said to her, "Whatever you want I'll give to you – even up to half my kingdom!" She went to her mother and asked her what she should ask for. "The head of John the Baptist," she answered with a smile.

The girl went back to the king with her request: "I want you to give me immediately the head of John the Baptist on a platter."

The king realised in his distress that he had promised too much, and everyone there had heard him make this promise so he could not back out; he also did not want to say no to her. He then sent an executioner to do the job, and very soon John's head was on a bloodied platter which Herod presented to Salome who gave it to her mother.

On hearing of John's death his disciples came and took his body and laid it in a tomb.

When Jesus heard what had happened, he left the crowds privately by boat to a secluded place.

The lives of John and Elijah did have similarities; they both appeared suddenly on the scene and spent much of their time in the wilderness. They both had an uncompromising message to give and Elijah clashed with the king. In Elijah's case, King Ahab's wife, Jezebel, wanted the prophet dead[25] but did not achieve it and Herodias desired to see John dead and in that she succeeded.

---

[25]   1 Kings 19:1-2

Food from the Messiah

Herod had heard of what Jesus had been doing and he was perplexed because some were saying that John had been raised from the dead, others that Elijah had appeared or one of the prophets of long ago had come back to life. Herod said, "I beheaded John. So who is this I'm hearing about?" Herod wanted to see this new prophet.

Although Jesus had privately taken himself away the crowds of people who had seen what miracles he had done did not want him to get away from them and so they followed him on foot to where he was. When Jesus saw how many there were he had compassion on them and healed their sick. It was getting close to evening and the disciples urged Jesus to send the people away so that they could go to the villages and buy some food.

Jesus said to Philip, "Where shall we buy food for these people?" He said this to test him because he already knew what he was going to do. Everything Jesus did and said had a profound significance that transcended its immediate effects. When he later spoke of the deeper meaning of food being provided free it proved to be so radical that many were offended by it and actually left him.

Philip answered, "Eight months wages wouldn't cover the cost of feeding all these people!" Andrew then pointed out the obvious, "Here's a boy with five small barley loaves and two small fish, but these titbits will make no difference." They were at a loss to know what to do.

"Make all these people sit down," Jesus said. Grass carpeted the ground and just counting the men brought the number up to 5,000. Jesus then took the boy's bread and fish, gave thanks and distributed to those who were reclining on the grass and there was enough food for all.

When the meal was finished the disciples gathered what was left which amounted to twelve full baskets. The people who had eaten this meal began to see Jesus as the Prophet who was to come, but Jesus, knowing that they intended to make him a ruler, by force if need be, left the area for the high ground by himself.

He had already sent the disciples into their boat to go ahead of him to the other side of the lake and he was alone praying. When it became dark the boat was getting into difficulties as the wind was against them and the waters were rough. Through the darkness and the cold spray of the crashing waves the figure of a man could be seen approaching their boat, and they were terrified and cried out in fear as whatever it was came closer.

"It's me, don't be afraid." It was the voice of Jesus but at that moment none of them could believe that it really was him.

"Lord," Peter called out, "if it's really you let me come to you on the water."

"Do it," Jesus said.

Peter slowly let himself down the side of the boat and to his and the other disciples' astonishment began to walk on the water towards Jesus. Peter gazed at the dark swelling waves, their edges torn by the strong wind, and looking down at his feet all he could think of was the madness of what he was doing and what he feared would happen began. He was beginning to go down and in the next moment he'd be under the waves. As he sank he shouted, "Lord, save me!"

Strong hands caught him and held him up and then he heard the familiar voice of Jesus, "Your faith ran out – why were you doubting?"

As they got into the boat the wind dropped. Shocked and open mouthed the disciples approached Jesus and fell to their knees, "You really are the son of God!"

Their minds went back to the other time they were crossing the lake when a furious squall developed and the waves were breaking over the boat and they realised that if it continued the boat was in danger of sinking. Jesus was on a cushion at the stern of the boat sleeping through the storm. They rushed over and woke him up, and he did not seem pleased to have his sleep disturbed. He rose and addressed the wind and sea as if they were his to command. "Quiet! Be still! And as obedient elements the wind died down and the water became calm.

"Why are you so afraid?" Jesus sternly addressed them, "You still don't have any trust."

Terrified, they asked each other, "Who is he? The wind and the waves even obey him!"

There were times when the disciples didn't understand what Jesus was saying and were afraid to ask him.[26]

---

[26]   Mark 9:32, Luke 18:34

The Messiah's real food and drink

"Rabbi," the crowds who had been fed had finally found him, "when did you get here?" They had travelled in a number of boats across the lake to Capernaum in search of him.

"You're looking for me not because you saw miraculous signs but because your stomachs were filled. Don't make all this effort for what is going to decay, but for food that lasts forever, which the Son of Man will give you. God the Father has placed his seal of approval on him."

"What does God require us to do?"

"The work of God is to believe in the one he has sent." Jesus answered.

"Give us some miraculous sign so we can see it and believe you. Our forefathers ate the manna[27] in the desert; as it's written; 'He gave them bread from heaven to eat.'"[28]

"I'm telling you the truth, it wasn't Moses who gave the bread from heaven, but it is my Father who gives you the true bread from heaven, because the bread of God is he who comes down from heaven and gives life to the world."

---

27   Manna means 'what is it?'

28   Exodus 16:4

"From now on please give us this bread," they asked him.

"I'm the bread of life. Whoever comes to me will never go hungry and those who believe in me will never be thirsty. But as I've told you before, you've seen me and you still don't believe. Everyone that the Father gives me will come to me and I'll never drive them away. None of them will be lost and I'll raise them up at the last day. Everyone whose focus is the Son and trusts him shall have eternal life."

What Jesus said ignited vocal criticism from them because Jesus identified himself as the bread from heaven and as they knew his family and where he grew up they concluded he did not and he could not have come down from heaven. Such an idea was madness.

"Stop complaining," Jesus answered. No-one can come to me unless the Father who sent me draws him, and I'll raise him up at the last day. Everyone who listens and learns from the Father comes to me. If you believe that I'm telling you the truth, you have eternal life.

"I'm the bread of life. Your forefathers ate the manna in the desert, yet they died, but here is the bread that comes down from heaven, which if a person eats they will not die. I'm the living bread; this bread is my flesh which I'll give for the life of the world.

"How can this man give us his flesh to eat?" they protested. The thought was repulsive.

Jesus went on to say, to his listener's horror, "Unless you can eat the flesh of the Son of Man and drink his blood, you'll have no life in you. My flesh is real food and my blood is real drink. Whoever eats my flesh and drinks my blood stays with me and I with him. In the same way as the living Father sent me and I live because of the Father, so the one who feeds on me will live because of me. Jesus said this while teaching in the synagogue in Capernaum.

This teaching was unacceptable for many of the disciples. "Does this offend you? What if the day comes when you see the Son of Man ascending back to heaven? The Spirit gives life; the flesh counts for nothing. The teaching I've given you is spiritual and they are life, but some of you don't believe."

From the beginning Jesus had known who wouldn't believe and who would betray him. At this time many of his disciples turned back and stopped following him.

Jesus turned to his twelve closest disciples and asked them, "Do you want to leave as well?"

"Lord, to whom shall we go?" Peter spoke for them all, "You have the words of eternal life; we believe and know that you are the Holy One of God."

"Have I not chosen you twelve? Yet one of you belongs to the adversary – Satan!"

After spending over three years in close proximity to Jesus, Judas Iscariot went to the chief priests with the determined intention of betraying Jesus. The high ranking priests were delighted to get this much wanted insider information and promised to reward him, and so he looked eagerly for an opportunity to have him arrested.

The family of the Messiah

Jesus was attracting many people who came to see what miracles he would do and to listen to what he had to say. Paradoxically his mother and his four brothers as well as his two sisters found the extra attention they were beginning to receive disturbing and they decided Jesus needed to be controlled as he didn't seem to be in his right mind. They left where they were and went to where he was because they wanted to limit any damage he might inadvertently cause by his unauthorised healings.[29]

The account is given that while Jesus and his disciples were at a house to speak to those gathered there, many others were attempting to enter so that they too could hear or even see the person who attracted so much controversy.

When his family who were nearby heard about this situation they were so concerned over what was happening that they came to the house with the intention of possibly rescuing Jesus from what could easily develop, in their minds, into a civil disturbance.

As they were unable to enter the house themselves they managed to get a message to Jesus while he was talking to those around him. When he learned that his mother, brothers and sisters were outside looking for him he said for everyone to hear, "Who is my mother and my brothers?" Looking around at those who were seated there he

---

[29]   Mark 3:21,31-32

continued, "Here are my mother and my brothers! Whoever listens to what God says and puts it into practice are my brother and sister and mother."

Another family event happened just prior to the Feast of Tabernacles[30]which almost everyone observed in the autumn. The brothers of Jesus said to him, "You should get down to Judea so that your followers can see your miracles, because if you want to become famous you mustn't hide yourself. Let the world see you." They too did not believe in him.

"The right time for me hasn't come," Jesus said to them, "but for you, any time is right. This world cannot hate you, but it hates me because I speak against those things that are evil. You go to the Feast. I'll go up later."

One of his brothers, James, later became the leader of the Jerusalem church,[31]and is the probable author of the letter of James. His other brother Jude also wrote a letter contained in Scripture. Mary, the mother of Jesus, is listed among the disciples who met together after his ascension. Jesus was amazed at the complete lack of belief he experienced in his home town. To them he was just a builder and a son of a builder who, along with his brothers and sisters, were familiar faces in the town, but familiarity wasn't the main reason they rejected him. He had told them something about God that they could not accept and it was a position that they shared with all the other people they knew.

That rejection concerned the Gentiles.

---

[30]   Lev 23:33-36

[31]   Gal 1:19

Jews and Gentiles

Some years later when the apostle Peter met Cornelius, a centurion of the Italian Regiment, at his home in Caesarea, he was faced not only with Cornelius but his relatives and friends. When Peter had entered the home of Cornelius, who generously gave to the poor and regularly prayed to God, he said to all those who were there, "You know very well that it's against our long and established tradition for a Jew to associate with a Gentile, but God has shown me that I shouldn't call anyone unclean."

When Peter returned to Jerusalem the circumcised believers criticised him saying, "You went into the house of uncircumcised men and ate with them." Peter then explained to them what had happened to cause him to break with what was almost a law amongst the Jews, and when they heard all the details their objections ended, and praising God they said, "We now see that God has even granted the Gentiles repentance to life."

But so deeply ingrained was the separation of Jews from Gentiles that even from the beginning of the formation of the church – the body of believers, many had great difficulties adjusting to this new way of thinking.

Some were teaching new Gentile Christians that unless they were circumcised according to the law taught by Moses, they couldn't be saved. It was then decided that this dispute needed to be settled by a special meeting at Jerusalem with the apostles and elders. At this meeting many of those who were Pharisees and believed in Jesus said, "The Gentiles must be circumcised and required to obey the law of Moses."

This heated debate went on until Peter reminded them of what happened with the conversion of Cornelius and that "God, who knows the heart, demonstrated that he accepted them by giving them the Holy Spirit, just as he did to us. God made no distinction between us and them, because he purified their hearts by faith. We believe that it's through the grace of our Lord Jesus that we're saved, just as they are." Paul and Barnabas also spoke of the miraculous signs that God had done through them for the Gentiles. James then quoted the prophet Amos where it is written, "After this I will return and rebuild David's fallen tent. Its ruins I will rebuild and I will restore it, that the remnant of men may seek the Lord, and the Gentiles who bear my name, says the Lord."[32]

Apparently those who had gone out teaching that new converts were to come under the law of Moses did it without any authorisation from the Jerusalem church so selected men were chosen to go to Antioch and read out the letter from the apostles reassuring them that circumcision was not a requirement for belonging to the body of Christ.

However, long held traditions have a way of hanging on as Paul was later to recount in his letter to the Galatians. "When Peter came to Antioch, I needed to set myself against what he was doing because it was wrong." Peter used to eat with the Gentiles but when some of those who supported the circumcision party arrived he separated himself from the Gentiles because he didn't want to be seen by this strict group enjoying a meal with them as he perhaps still felt uncomfortable socialising with those he had always been separate from.

---

[32] From the Septuagint: the Greek translation of the Hebrew Scriptures.

The results of his insincerity were that other Jews joined him and stopped eating with the Gentiles. Peter was in fear of this pressure group and he gave in. Paul wrote, "When I saw that they were not acting in line with the truth of the gospel, I said to Peter in front of them all, 'You are a Jew, yet you live like a Gentile and not a Jew. So how is it that you force Gentiles to follow Jewish customs? We who are Jews by birth and not, as the saying goes, Gentile sinners, know that a man isn't justified by observing the law but by faith in Jesus Christ because by observing the law no-one will be justified."

Throughout his travels Paul was attacked because he taught that circumcision wasn't necessary and that attempting to be justified before God by the keeping of the law puts us under the law and condemned by the same law. In fact the law then becomes a curse because it shows us our guilt before God but as Paul wrote, 'Christ redeemed us from the curse of the law by becoming a curse for us,'[33]

Paul went on to write concerning his fellow Jews who were hostile to his message, 'What shall we say then? That the Gentiles, who didn't pursue righteousness, have obtained it – a righteousness that is by faith; but Israel, who did pursue a law of righteousness, didn't obtain it. Why didn't they? Because they pursued it by works (what they did and were able to accomplish) instead of faith. They fell at the stone, as it's written, "See, I lay in Zion a stone that causes men to trip and a rock that makes them fall, but the one who trusts in him will never be put to shame."[34] Paul went on to say, 'they are zealous for God but their zeal isn't based on knowledge. Because they didn't know the righteousness that comes from God and attempted to establish their own, they didn't submit to God's righteousness.'[35]

---

[33]   Gal 3:13

[34]   Isa 8:14, 28:16

[35]   Rom 9:31-33, 10:1-3

Jesus had said to the religious leaders, "Have you never read in the Scriptures: 'the stone the builders rejected has become the capstone, the Lord has done this, and it's marvellous to see.' Because of your rejection of me the kingdom of God will be taken away from you and given to a people who respond positively to my teaching. He who falls on this stone will be broken to pieces and he on whom it falls will be crushed."[36]

Jesus spent much of his time in Galilee which was a fulfilment of what Isaiah had written – 'Land of Zebulun and land of Naphtali[37]the way to the sea, along the Jordan, Galilee of the Gentiles – the people living in darkness have seen a great light; on those living in the land of the shadow of death a light has dawned.'[38]

Jesus was alone when he entered the synagogue at Nazareth, as his custom was, and the scroll of the prophet Isaiah was given to him to read. Unrolling it he found the place where it is written, 'The Spirit of the Lord is on me, because he has anointed me to peach good news to the poor. He has sent me to proclaim freedom for the prisoners and recovery of sight for the blind, to release the oppressed, to proclaim the year of the Lord's favour.'

When he finished the reading he rolled up the scroll and passed it back to the attendant and sat down. Everyone in that synagogue was looking at him because he spoke as one who had authority, and then he said, "What you've just heard is being fulfilled today."

At that point they were listening and marvelled because they knew him as the son of the builder, Joseph, so how, they thought, can he make such a claim of greatness?

---

[36]   Matt 21:42-44

[37]   Originally it was where two of the tribes of Israel settled after coming out of Egypt.

[38]   Isa 9:1-2

His words had fallen on the hard soil of firmly held attitudes and they began to show by their expressions how little impact his words had made.

He said to them, "I'm sure you'll quote the proverb, 'physician, heal yourself!' Do the same things here in your home town that you've been doing over in Capernaum. I'm telling you the truth, no prophet is accepted in his own town." Because of their hardness of heart he tells them what God did in their own national history. "There were many widows in Israel in Elijah's time, when there was a drought over the whole land for three and a half years, yet Elijah wasn't sent to any of them, but a widow living near Sidon, a Gentile region. And there were many in Israel with leprosy in the time of Elisha the prophet, yet none of them was cleansed except for Naaman the Syrian."

Jesus was referring to one of the many times in Israel's history when paganism was common place and how in such times God chose to show his power outside of Israel. The people in the synagogue were furious when they heard of God's kindness to the Gentiles. They took him outside to the edge of a steep hill and were about to throw him down but somehow he was able to walk right through the crowd and then left the area. They had rejected him and so he rejected them and never returned to Nazareth.

Jesus sent out his disciples and gave them authority to drive out evil spirits and to heal every disease and sickness, but before they left he instructed them not to go among the Gentiles or enter any town of the Samaritans; they were to go to the spiritually lost of Israel and tell them that the Kingdom of God is near.

For that limited period of time that he was to be with them the priority must be Israel first, but it was inevitable that he would come into contact with Gentiles and when he did their response would surprise him.

Jesus was on the outskirts of Capernaum when some of the leaders of the Jews came to him requesting that he would heal the servant of a centurion who was close to death. The centurion had a great respect for his servant who was ill, and he loved their nation and had built a synagogue for them and so the leaders were earnest in their request that Jesus go immediately to this man's house.

Jesus agreed to go and when they were near the house a servant came to him with a message from the centurion, 'Lord, there's no need for you to come into my house and I don't consider myself worthy to come to you, but I know that if you just say the word my servant will be healed. I'm under authority and I have soldiers under my authority – what I tell them to do – they do.' This amazing display of faith took Jesus' breath away and he said to the servant, "Go! Tell him that it will be done just as he believed it would." Turning to the crowd he said, "I haven't found such great faith even in this country which should be filled with faithful people." Those who gave Jesus the centurion's message returned to the house and found the servant well.

Jesus and his disciples entered the Gentile area of Tyre and Sidon. It was a private visit and he didn't want it known that he was there, but his presence was soon known about and a Greek woman came to him addressing him as Son of David, one of the titles of the coming Messiah. She pleaded for her daughter who was suffering from demon-possession. As she repeatedly asked him for help and Jesus was not answering her request, his disciples urged him to do something as she kept up her desperate pleading. "I was sent to the lost sheep of Israel." Jesus finally said to her.

Kneeling before him she implored him, "Lord, help me."

"It's not right to take the children's bread and toss it to their dogs." The Jews had contempt for the Gentiles and referred to them as dogs, but Jesus had no contempt in his voice.

"That's true Lord," she answered, "but even the dogs get to eat whatever crumbs that fall from their masters' table."

"Woman, you have great faith; your request is granted, the demon has left your daughter." When she got home her little girl was lying on the bed, and the demon had gone.

Much later Paul was to write a letter to the Christians at Ephesus in which he said, 'Remember that formerly you who are Gentiles by birth and called 'uncircumcised' by those who call themselves 'the circumcised' and at that time you were apart and separate from Christ, excluded from citizenship in Israel – foreigners to the covenants of the promise – without hope and without God in the world. But now in the Messiah Jesus you who were far away are near through his blood.

'He is our peace, who has made the two, Gentiles and Jews, one, and has destroyed that barrier – that dividing wall of hostility, by abolishing in his body the law with its commandments and regulations. His reason for doing this was to create in his likeness one new man out of the two; in this way he has made peace and has reconciled both of them to God through the cross, which was how that deep hostility of theirs was put to death. To both, those who were near and those who were far away he came and taught peace, and because of what he did both Gentiles and Jews have access to the Father by one Spirit.'[39]Paul goes on to write, 'As a result of this you Gentiles are no longer foreigners and aliens, but fellow citizens with God's people and members of God's household, built on the foundation of the apostles and prophets, with the Messiah himself as the chief corner stone. We are joined together in him and are growing into a holy temple. We are being remade together so that God can live in us by his Spirit.'

Speaking to a Samaritan woman was something Jews were not expected to do, yet Jesus made a simple and profound statement to

---

[39]   Eph 2:11-22

her that "God is Spirit,"[40]so that when his Spirit is within a person they are sharing a degree of God's nature and mind, just as our spirit is our mind and nature. This is the seal that believers are marked with – the promised Holy Spirit. That Spirit is of and from God and is a deposit guaranteeing our inheritance until the resurrection when all the believers will be changed from mortal to immortal. [41]

Paul underlines this historic development in his letter to the Galatians, 'You're all sons of God through faith and trust in the Messiah, because all of you who were baptised into him have clothed yourselves with him. In him, whether Jew or Greek, slave or free, male or female, none of these differences matter because you're all one in him, and if you belong to him then you're a descendant of Abraham and heirs according to the promise.'[42]

As children of Abraham by faith, Christians have inherited the promise that God gave him, saying, "All nations will be blessed through you," referring to the Messiah. That birth into this family of faith does not happen naturally but to those who believe and trust in the Messiah he has given them the right to become children of God – children born not of natural descent, nor of human decision, or a husbands will, but born of God.[43]

---

[40]   John 4:24

[41]   Eph 1:13b-14

[42]   Gal 3:26-29.

[43]   John 1: 12-13

Only two groups

The apostle John in his second letter writes of how great is the love the Father has lavished on us, that we should be called children of God, and that is what we are. And John goes on to say that we know who the children of God are and who the children of the devil are.

We either belong to God or we belong to the devil. John also wrote, 'We know that we are children of God and that the whole world is under the control of the evil one.' Jesus called him the 'prince of this world' unseen but real, and the one who offered the world to Jesus if only he would accept his evil rule and subject himself to him.

Jesus made this distinction clear when giving an answer to the disciples who asked him why he spoke in parables to the people. In speaking in parables he was fulfilling a part of one of the psalms which says, "I will open my mouth in parables, I will utter things hidden since the creation of the world."[44] But there was a greater reason why he spoke in parables. He said to his disciples, "The knowledge of the secrets of the kingdom of God has been given to you," (Jesus was telling them that the choice and initiative for them to be called to be disciples came not from them but from God) "but not to them. Whoever has will be given more and he'll have plenty, but those who don't have, even what they have will be taken from them. This is why I speak to them in parables." [45]

---

[44]   Psa 78:2

[45]   Matt 13:10-17

In the accounts of God sending a prophet to speak to his people they have always and consistently been met with hostility. Jeremiah spoke right up to the time when the city of Jerusalem fell and its people taken into captivity. His message was that this disaster was avoidable. "Announce this to the house of Jacob and proclaim it in Judah: Listen to this you foolish and senseless people, who have eyes but don't see, who have ears but don't hear: shouldn't you fear me? Shouldn't you tremble in my presence? But these people have stubborn and rebellious hearts; they've turned aside and gone away."

Jeremiah went on to say, "To whom can I speak and give warning? Who will listen to me? Their ears are closed so that they cannot hear. The word of the Lord is offensive to them; they find no pleasure in it."

Isaiah experienced the same response from the people and he was inspired to write, "Go and tell this people: 'Be ever hearing, but never understanding; be ever seeing, but never perceiving. Make the heart of this people calloused; make their ears dull and close their eyes. Otherwise (if only they had a better attitude) they might see with their eyes, hear with their ears, understand with their hearts, and turn and be healed.'

Jesus quoted this prophecy of Isaiah to his disciples explaining that the people he spoke to shared the same attitude as those Jeremiah and Isaiah faced. "But blessed are your eyes because they see," Jesus told them, "and your ears because they hear. I'm telling you the truth, many prophets and righteous men longed to see what you see but didn't see it, and to hear what you hear but didn't hear it."

Jesus explained this division between those who did not want to hear and those who did privately to his disciples, and the analogy he used in his speaking to the people concerned various types of soil that either worked well for the seed planted in it or did not.

The seed that fell on hardened ground did not stand a chance of taking root which was an illustration of the many who hear the message of the kingdom of God and none of it sinks in.

The seed that fell on rocky ground where there was not much soil stood for those who did receive the message but it did not go very deep and when problems came they gave it up.

The seed that was planted among the thorns and could not survive pictures the person whose ears are open to the message but the worries of this life, the deceitfulness of wealth and the desires for other things come in and choke the message.

And then there is the seed planted in good soil that pictures a person who not only hears the message but puts it into practice and remains faithful.

Jesus used language that was plain and understandable to people but its spiritual significance in most cases was lost on them, not because of Jesus but on account of the hardness of their own hearts.

Many of the parables concerned the kingdom of God and began with 'the kingdom of God is like...' a field that was sown with good seed, but while everyone was sleeping the enemy of the planter came and planted weeds among the wheat and then went away. When the wheat began to grow it was obvious that weeds were all over the field and the owner's workmen wondered where these weeds came from.

"An enemy did this," the owner replied.

"Shall we go and pull the weeds out?" the servants asked.

"Don't do that, because as you're pulling out the weeds you're likely to pull up the wheat as well, so let them both grow together until the harvest and then I'll instruct the harvesters to first collect the weeds and tie them into bundles to be burned; then gather the wheat and take it into my barn."

Then Jesus went into a house with his disciples, who like the crowd who heard this parable, didn't know what it meant, and they wanted to know and so they asked him to explain it to them. This was the difference between the disciples and the others – they wanted to understand. As Jesus came to the end of the parable he said, "He who has ears, let him hear." Listening and asking questions were crucial to finding the truth contained within the parable.

Jesus explained the parable to his disciples, and yet so much misleading teaching has been poured over it that even the explanations that are commonly held have to be de-weeded.

Jesus told them that "The one who sowed the good seed is the Son of Man and the field is the world. The good seed stands for the sons of the kingdom and the weeds are the sons of the evil one. The enemy who sows them is the devil. The harvest is the end of the age and the harvesters are angels.

"At the end of the age the Son of Man will send his angels and they will weed out of his kingdom everything and everyone that causes sin and they'll be thrown into the blazing furnace, where there will be weeping and gnashing of teeth. Then the righteous will shine like the sun in the kingdom of their Father."

Many think in terms of the end of the world when Christ returns but that is never said, what is said, and twice in this parable alone, is the end of this age. The world does continue but the age to come will be ruled over by the kingdom of God with Jesus at its head.

This super-heated furnace is the same blazing fire that Malachi wrote of; "Surely the day is coming; it will burn like a furnace. All the arrogant and every evildoer will be stubble, and that day that is coming will set them on fire. Not a root or branch will be left to them. But for you who revere my name, the sun of righteousness will rise with healing in its wings, and you will go out and leap like calves released from the stall. Then you will trample down the wicked; they will be ashes under the soles of your feet on the day when I do these things," says the Lord Almighty. [46]

John the Baptist spoke of the one who was to follow him, "His winnowing fork is in his hand, and he will clear his threshing-floor, gathering his wheat into the barn and burning up the chaff with unquenchable fire."[47] In none of these pictures of a future judgment that John and Jesus used is the idea that somehow those who are thrown into this furnace and reduced to ashes are still alive and continue to suffer eternally.

Some very influential teachers claim, without any biblical support, that the wicked are given super eternal bodies that can survive the fire, and so continue to endure the pain of the flames but never die. This teaching finds its origin in writings outside of the Bible and yet is accepted by millions as true.

But what about those words of Jesus himself? When he said, "Their worm does not die and the fire is not quenched."[48] Those words were not made up by Jesus; they are a quote from the very end of the book of Isaiah which says, in full; "And they will go out and look upon the dead bodies of those who rebelled against me; their worm will not die, nor will their fire be quenched, and they will be loathsome to all mankind."[49]

---

[46]   Mal 4: 1-3.

[47]   Matt 3: 12

[48]   Mark 9:48

[49]   Isa 66: 24

Questions should have been asked concerning this worm, as this infamous invertebrate is always mentioned as a part of the ongoing torture that the wicked endure throughout eternity, but it is never mentioned how much of the victim they actually eat, or is it a continually gnawing and nibbling around the edges until there is nothing left? But that cannot be right, as this tragic individual lives forever in the dark and fire and wouldn't their strengthened asbestos bodies give them immunity from these immortal worms?

Such nonsense is the logical outcome of inventing a teaching that is a distortion of what Jesus said and meant. His quote from Isaiah was referring to dead bodies rotting away and covered with maggots. This was the fate of criminals who were put to death in his time and before. The Valley of Hinnom which was south-west of Jerusalem had a dreadful history.

In Old Testament times this deep narrow depression was a place of child sacrifice in worship of Molech or Milcom, a Cannanite deity. Child sacrifices were also made to Baal, to the host of heaven and to other foreign gods.[50] This site gained the epithet of an accursed place and it became a place for dumping corpses and other refuse.[51] During the time prior to Jesus there developed the idea that this valley would be the place of the fiery destruction of the wicked.

Gehenna is a word from the Hebrew meaning 'valley of Hinnom' and is routinely translated in the Bible as 'hell.' The teaching that this valley stood for the final state of torment for the wicked can be traced only from non-biblical sources such as *First Enoch, The Apocalypse of Zephaniah, The Gospel of Nicodemus, The Apocalypse of Peter* and *The Fourth Book of Maccabees 13:14-15*, and other apocryphal literature. With the exception of James 3:6, the word Gehenna only occurs in the teaching of Jesus where it's apparent that Jesus assumed

---

[50]   Jer 32:35. 2 kings 23:10. 2 Chr 28:3, 33:6. Jer 7:31-32, 19:2,6.

[51]   Jer 19:6-7.

his hearers would understand what was meant by Gehenna. While Gehenna is translated as 'hell' in most English versions, we must take care not to read back into the NT ideas of 'hell' that developed only much later in Christian theology.[52]

The teaching of everlasting torment owes more to the writings of Virgil and Dante than to the Scriptures.[53]

As being thrown into a furnace would quickly reduce anything to ashes the 'weeping and gnashing of teeth' that Jesus spoke of takes place when the reality of seeing those who are inside of the kingdom, while they themselves are on the outside hits home and produces in them a great emotional distress and anger at hearing that their fate is to be a permanent and everlasting destruction.[54] The words 'destruction' and 'destroy' are used many times in connection with the fate of the wicked. It is the fate of Satan and his demons to suffer for an eternity but he has successfully deceived the majority of Christians into accepting the lie of eternal suffering for condemned humans.

Others will point to the parable of the rich man and Lazarus as proof of continual suffering in hell, but they ignore that this is an example story about the deceitfulness of riches, not a teaching on the fate of the wicked. In fact Jesus doesn't even use the word Gehenna here but the word Hades (the place of the dead). This story is in the context of warnings directed at the rich who store things up for themselves but are not rich towards to God.

Jesus had mentioned that the Pharisees who loved money were the ones who justified themselves in the eyes of men, but, to their sneers and anger, he said to them, "what is highly valued among men is

---

[52]   See the Lutterworth Dictionary of the Bible. p. 319

[53]   Excerpt of a letter from Michael Green to the author.

[54]   Rev 20:11-15.

detestable in God's sight." The story of a man who had all he wanted and a man who had nothing was an effective way of teaching that repentance and change was something to do now rather than attempt it when it was too late, as in this story the rich man made no changes to his life while he lived and found to his deep distress that the time for change had gone.

This negative example story is about the misuse of resources and the great spiritual danger which that selfish attitude leads to. Even though on the outside he looked to be in a much better place than Lazarus, there was going to be a huge reversal of condition when the unavoidable judgment came and the futility of trying to negotiate his way out of his distress. It's a story of learning a lesson too late and a warning to his listeners to repent now and not later. Our heart will be where our treasure is.

The English word 'hell' comes unchanged from Old English (cf. Old Norse *Hel*, goddess of the dead). The King James Version of 1611 uses the word 'hell' to translate the Hebrew word 'Sheol' – place of the dead or the grave, and the Greek word which carries the same meaning, 'Hades' is also translated as hell in that, and other versions. These words and the word Gehenna need to be examined individually and in context.

The wages of sin is not eternal life in hell but the second and permanent death from which there is no further resurrection. To believe that God would torture people for an eternity would make him into a monster; God would not do that but our enemy Satan has led millions of us to believe that God would torture the unsaved eternally.

John writes about this second death in speaking of the first and second resurrection; "They (those belonging to the Messiah) came to life and reigned with Christ for a thousand years. The rest of the dead did not come to life until the thousand years were ended. This is the first resurrection.

"Blessed and holy are those who have part in the first resurrection. The second death has no power over them, but they will be priests of God and of Christ and will reign with him for a thousand years." A little further on John writes, "The dead were judged according to what they had done as recorded in the books. The sea gave up the dead that were in it, and death and Hades (the grave) gave up the dead that were in them, and each person was judged according to what he had done. Then death and the grave were thrown into the lake of fire. The lake of fire is the second death. If anyone's name was not found written in the book of life, he was thrown into the lake of fire."[55]

This symbolic language tells us that there will come a time when death is no more and those who do not belong to God will also be no more.

---

[55]   Rev 20:4b-6, 12b-15

The shut door

Jesus was reminded by a number of people about the Galileans[56]whose spilt blood Pilate had mixed with their sacrifices, and was asked if he thought that because of the way they died it was evidence that they were worse sinners than others, and Jesus said to them, "Don't think that because of the way they died that proved they were worse sinners than others, because I tell you, unless you repent you too will all perish."

Jesus then brings up a natural disaster where eighteen people died when the tower in Siloam collapsed on them. Siloam was the location of a water reservoir for Jerusalem on the south and east walls of the city. These different ways of dying really made no difference in the matter of the need for repentance because if that is not there, we will, as he said, perish.

Then, as his habit was, he told a parable. "A man had a fig-tree in his vineyard, and he came to look for fruit on it but didn't find any. He told the person who took care of the vineyard, 'For the last three years I've been coming here looking for fruit but haven't found any so cut it down – it's taking up valuable space.' The man thought it should be given a bit more time and suggested that they leave it for one more year, and during that time he will dig round it and fertilise it and if it bears fruit next year, great! But if it doesn't, then cut it down."

---

[56]   Luke 13:1

Unless some good fruit is seen it will not last much longer. John had warned those religious Pharisees and the secular Sadducees coming to see him, "You brood of vipers! Who warned you to run from the coming wrath? Produce fruit in keeping with repentance."

Jesus then went to the towns and villages, all the time teaching as he journeyed towards Jerusalem. On the way someone asked him if only a few people are going to be saved. He naturally wanted to know numbers and percentages. The general feeling was that Israel would be saved and perhaps a few exceptional Gentiles but salvation was, as they believed, reserved for those descended from Abraham. Jesus turns the attention away from national aspirations and numbers to the individual.

"Make every effort to enter through the narrow door; many will try to enter and will not be able to. Once the owner of the house closes the door you'll be standing knocking and pleading for the door to be opened. But the answer will come back, "I don't recognise you or where you've come from."

"But, we ate and drank with you," they argued, "and you taught in our streets."

"I still don't know you – get away from here you evil doers! There will be anguish and rage when you see Abraham, Isaac and Jacob and all the prophets in the kingdom of God and you thrown out. People will come from around the world and take their places at the feast in the kingdom of God. Those you think will be there won't be and those you think won't be there will be."

Jesus emphasised the same urgency of acting on what you hear and being prepared to take the harder route when there exists what seems to be a far easier way. "Enter through the narrow gate, for wide is the gate and broad is the road that leads to destruction, and many go that way. But the gate that leads to life is small and narrow and only a few find it."

"Not everyone who says to me Lord," Jesus went on to say, "will enter the kingdom of heaven[57] but only those who do the will of my Father who's in heaven. Many will say to me on that day, 'Lord, didn't we prophesy in your name, and in your name drive out demons and perform many miracles?'

"But I'll tell them, 'I never knew you; get away from me you evildoers.'"

The shut door image plainly allows us to see that a time limit exists where it will be too late even for those who looked as though they had a close relationship with Jesus but were in fact far from him. The time limit isn't his return but the duration of our lives, and as none of us know how long we have left to live, it is of the greatest importance that we act now on what we know – before it's too late.

Following Jesus demands a determined focus and total commitment. It will take accepting being last and embracing rejection. It may even mean standing up for what you believe is true even though your Christian brothers and sisters think you are following heresy by going against traditional teaching. Being a disciple of Jesus makes a person an alien in a hostile environment – as lambs among wolves.

A man came up to Jesus expressing the commitment to follow Jesus wherever he goes, but Jesus, instead of welcoming him, said, "Foxes have holes and birds have nests but the Son of Man doesn't have a home."

Another man received an invitation from Jesus to follow him, but the man answered, "Lord, first I have to bury my father."

---

[57]   Matthew uses the word heaven in deference to Jewish sensibility over using the word God.

"Let the dead bury their own dead, you are to go and proclaim the kingdom of God."

"I will follow you," another said to him, "but first let me go back and say good-bye to my family."

"No-one who puts his hand to the plough and looks back is fit for service in the kingdom of God." Proclaiming the kingdom of God and seeking his righteousness must come first.

The religious establishment

"He's a blasphemer and a deceiver making claims no man should make. His healings are only possible because he's tapping in to Satan's power and he's a glutton and a wino[58]what's more, he criticizes us – the separated ones – we who diligently study the Scriptures and publicly pray for our nation's good. He undermines our traditions, customs and the way we worship – he needs to be got rid of and the sooner the better!"

Not all the religious elite thought that way; some even believed in him but were afraid to go public with their convictions as they would have quickly lost their position of respect and the privileges that went with it.

One of the ruling council members, Nicodemus, visited Jesus during the night and spoke to him respectfully, calling him Rabbi, "We know you are a teacher who has come from God, for no-one could perform the miraculous signs you're doing if God wasn't with you."

Here is a man who was waiting for the kingdom of God to arrive and perhaps he saw in Jesus the beginning of that kingdom.

---

[58]   The temperance movement that many Christians approve of has no biblical warrant. The Bible condemns the abuse of alcohol, not its use. See Isaiah 25:6.

"I'm telling you the truth," Jesus replied to him, "no-one can see the kingdom of God unless they're born again."

"How can they be born again when they're adults?" Nicodemus countered, failing to understand that Jesus wasn't talking about a physical rebirth.

"No-one can enter the kingdom of God unless he's born of water and the Spirit." As Nicodemus studied the Scriptures he might have thought at that moment of the words that Ezekiel wrote; "I will sprinkle clean water on you and you will be clean; I'll cleanse you from all your impurities and from all your idols. I'll give you a new heart and put a new spirit in you and I'll remove your heart of stone and give you a heart of flesh."[59] "Flesh gives birth to flesh," Jesus continued, "but the Spirit gives birth to spirit. Don't be surprised when I say, 'You must be born again from above' the wind blows from all directions; you can hear it but you can't say where it comes from or where it's going. It's the same with all those who are born of the Spirit."

"How can this happen?" Nicodemus was puzzled. He knew the Scriptures but he had never heard this radical change of heart put in such a way before and he still did not realise what Jesus meant. This was new to him.

"You are Israel's teacher and you don't understand these things? We speak of what we know and what we've seen, but you still don't accept it. I have spoken to you of physical things and you don't believe; how then will you believe if I speak of spiritual things? I'm telling you the truth; no-one has ever gone into heaven except the one who came from there – the Son of Man. (heaven is always spoken in Scripture as where Jesus came from, never as the place Christians are going to) As Moses lifted up the bronze snake in the desert, so that those who looked at it could be healed from their deadly snake

---

[59]   Ezek 36: 25-26

bites,[60] so the Son of Man must be lifted up and everyone who looks and believes in him will have eternal life."

Often the Pharisees would come to him and test him with questions such as asking for a sign from heaven, and Jesus said to them, "This is a wicked generation. It asks for a miraculous sign but none will be given it except the sign of Jonah. Jonah was a sign to the Ninevites and so also will the Son of Man be to this generation. The Queen of the South will rise at the judgment with those of this generation and condemn them. She came a great distance to listen to Solomon's wisdom and now one greater than Solomon is here. The inhabitants of Nineveh will stand at the judgment with this generation and condemn it, because they repented at the preaching of Jonah, and now one greater than Jonah is here."

His own disciples often did not grasp his meaning when he used figurative language. There was a time when they were all in a boat crossing the Sea of Galilee when Jesus said to them, "Be careful to watch out for the yeast of the Pharisees and that of Herod. As they only had one piece of bread with them they thought Jesus was referring in some way to the fact that they were short of bread.

Jesus, aware of what they were talking about asked them, "Why are you talking about having no bread? Do you still not see or understand? Are your hearts hardened? Do you have eyes but fail to see, and ears but fail to hear. I wasn't talking to you about bread but to be on your guard against the yeast of the Pharisees and the Sadducees." Then it clicked that Jesus' point was to be alert to the teaching of the religious establishment.

They had experienced a continuing conflict with the religious groups over the way Jesus was leading them. Some Pharisees and teachers of the law came all the way from Jerusalem and queried

---

[60]   Num 21:4-9

Jesus as to why his disciples were breaking the tradition of the elders by not washing their hands[61]before they ate.

"And why do you break the command of God," Jesus hits back at them, "for the sake of your tradition? For God said, 'Honour your father and mother' and 'Anyone who curses his father or mother must be put to death,'[62]but you say that if a man says to his parents, 'Whatever financial support you might have received from me is now a gift devoted to God and you have no right to it.' In doing this, through a legal loophole, you nullify the word of God by your tradition. You hypocrites! Isaiah was right when he wrote about you: "These people honour me with their lips, but their hearts are far from me. They worship me in vain; their teachings are nothing but man-made rules."[63]

"Listen and understand," Jesus said to the crowd that had gathered, "What goes into a man's mouth doesn't make him 'unclean' but what comes out of his mouth makes him 'unclean.'"

"Do you realise that what you said offended the Pharisees," the disciples informed Jesus.

"Every plant that my heavenly Father hasn't planted will be pulled up by the roots. Leave them; they're blind guides and if a blind man leads a blind man they'll both fall into a pit."

"Explain this parable to us," Peter asked expectantly.

"Are you still so dull-headed?" Jesus said to all of them.

---

[61] This ceremonial hand washing came from later Jewish tradition, not from Old Testament law.

[62] Exodus 20: 12. 21:17, Lev 20:9.

[63] Isa 29:13

"Don't you see that whatever goes in your mouth goes into the stomach and is then it's eliminated in the normal way? But those things that come out of your mouth come from your heart, and it's these things that make a person 'unclean'. It's out of your heart those 'unclean' thoughts come. Thoughts of murder, adultery, sexual immorality, theft, lies and misrepresentation but eating without washing your hands doesn't make you 'unclean'"

One of the greatest offences that Jesus committed in the eyes of the religious groups was his conduct over the Sabbath. There was the time when he walked through the cornfields and as his disciples were hungry they picked some of the ears of corn and began to eat them. This involved the picking, rubbing the corn in their hands and throwing away the husks. These could be, and were, interpreted as reaping, threshing and winnowing and perhaps, considering that they ate the corn, their preparation of the corn would have to be taken into consideration as well!

The *Mishnah*[64] had thirty-nine prohibitions specifically concerning the Sabbath! These traditional rules were known as 'the forty save one'. Using these rules the disciples were guilty of breaking at least three of them.

Armed with these serious infringements they drew Jesus' attention to what his disciples were doing. "Look! What there're doing is illegal on the Sabbath."

Jesus doesn't address directly what his disciples were doing but took these critics on a history lesson where the letter of the law was not kept by the greatest king in their past. "Haven't you read what David did when he and those with him were hungry?" He then related how David and his men, who were outcasts at that time and on the run from King Saul, were helped by Ahimelech the priest who gave

---

[64]   The word means 'to repeat'. It began as oral law that amplified and added to the law of Moses.

them some of the consecrated bread which was freshly baked and was intended to replace the bread that had been on a special table close to the ark of the covenant for the past week. This was strictly for the use of the Levites.[65] (Ahimelech and the priests with him were later to be killed by Saul for helping David).

Then Jesus referred to the amount of work the priests had to do each Sabbath but because they were serving in the temple their work was legitimate. "I'm telling you," Jesus was about to make a statement that would be taken by his enemies as blasphemy, "that one greater than the temple is here. You need to know and understand what Hosea meant when he said, 'I desire mercy, not sacrifice'[66]and then you wouldn't have condemned the innocent. What my disciples did, they did on my authority because the Son of Man is Lord of the Sabbath."

A week later Jesus was in their synagogue and saw a man there who had a paralysed hand, and the Pharisees there were looking at Jesus to see if he'd heal this man, and if he did they could accuse him of breaking the Sabbath. Their law said that you could only treat someone if their life was in danger.[67] Jesus spoke directly to the man who had the damaged hand, "Stand up in front of everyone." Turning to all the others there he asked them, "Tell me what is lawful to do on the Sabbath: to do good or to do evil, to save life or to kill?" No answer came from those there. He looked at them in anger and deeply distressed at their stubborn attitudes he said to the man, "Stretch out your hand." As he did this everyone could see that his hand was completely healed. Immediately the Pharisees left the building and plotted with the Herodians as to how they could kill Jesus.

---

65   1 Sam 21:1-6. 22:11-23

66   Hosea 6:6

67   Mishnah *Yoma* 8:6

He knew what they intended so he left that area and many people followed him. As he healed those of them who were suffering from various health problems, including demon possession, the spirits recognised who he was and they loudly said to him, "You are the Son of God," but he warned these spirits to be silent and not to tell who he was.

Isaiah had written: "Here is my servant whom I've chosen, the one I love, in whom I delight; I will put my Spirit on him, and he'll proclaim justice to the nations. He'll not quarrel or shout out; no-one will hear his voice in the streets. That which is very weak he'll not break and those with little strength he'll be gentle with, until he leads them to justice and victory on earth. In his name the nations will put their trust."[68]

When Jesus was on a visit to Jerusalem he saw a man lying by a pool which was called 'the house of mercy.'[69] This man was unable to get himself into the pool as it was thought that when the water was disturbed whoever got in first would be healed. This disturbance may have occurred because of the occasional bubbling up of a natural spring. There were two pools there which were part of a large reservoir system and they were surrounded by five covered colonnades. In speaking to the man Jesus discovered that he had been coming there for the past thirty-eight years. There were many who suffered serious disabilities that waited there for the water to be disturbed.

"Do you want to get well?" Jesus asked the man.

"I've no-one to help me into the pool when it's disturbed, so somebody else always gets in before me," he spoke with frustration.

---

[68]   Isa 42: 1-4

[69]   *Bethesda*

"Get on your feet," Jesus gave the command simply, "take your mat and walk." Immediately the man was healed. He did as he was told and began to walk, but religious Jews seeing him carrying his mat confronted him with his obvious violation of the Sabbath.

"It's the Sabbath! The law forbids you to carry your mat."

"But the man who made me well told me to pick it up and walk."

"Who told you to walk with your mat?" they asked.

The healed man had no idea who it was because Jesus had left the area. Later Jesus saw him at the temple and said to him, "Now that you're well stop sinning and be reconciled to God or something much worse than the disability you had will come to you."

Once the man knew the name of Jesus he went straight to those who wanted to know the identity of the man who healed him and told them what they wanted to know.

Because Jesus continued to do these healings on the Sabbath the religious leaders were incensed and went after him hoping to arrest him. Jesus said to them in answer to their allegation of breaking the Sabbath, "My Father is always working just as I do." At this his critics wanted him dead because he was calling God his own Father and that made himself equal with God.

To this Jesus added, "The truth of my relationship with my Father is that the Son can't do anything by himself – it's only by seeing what the Father does that the Son can do anything. The Father who loves the Son shows him what to do. Just as the Father gives life to the dead so the Son gives life to whoever he's pleased to give it to. All judgment has now been entrusted to the Son. Anyone who doesn't honour the Son doesn't honour the Father who sent him. The person who listens to what I say and believes the One who sent me has eternal life and will not be condemned because he's crossed over from death to life."

At the same time Jesus said to them, "I'm telling you the truth – the time has now come when the dead will hear the voice of the son of God and they will live. As the father has life, and all life comes from him, so he has given the Son that same self-existent life and has given him authority to judge because of who he is.[70]Don't be amazed at what I'm saying because the time is coming when all who are in their graves will hear his voice and rise – some to eternal life and others to be condemned. I can do nothing by myself but I judge as I hear and my judgment is just because I'm not looking to please myself but the One who sent me.

"I can't witness for myself – it wouldn't be lawful – but there is another who speaks for me and I know that this witness about me is valid. You sent your questions to John and he spoke the truth concerning me, not that I'm looking for human testimony, but I'm saying this so that you may be saved. John was a lamp that burned and gave light, and for a while you enjoyed his light, yet I have a greater message than John and this is the work that the Father has sent me to finish which I'm doing. He himself speaks about me, but you've never heard his voice or seen his form, neither does his word find room in you because you don't believe the one he sent.

"You study diligently the Scriptures because you think that by just reading them you have eternal life. These scriptures that you so carefully read speak about me, but you refuse to come to me to have life.

"I don't accept praise from people, but I know you and that you don't have the love of God in your hearts. I've come in my Father's name and you don't accept me, yet if someone else comes in his own name you'll accept him. How can you believe when you accept each

---

[70]   Dan 7:13-14

other's praise yet make no effort to gain the praise that comes from God alone?

"Don't think that I'll accuse you before the Father. Your accuser is Moses; you set your hopes on him, but if you believed Moses you would believe me because he wrote about me, but since you don't believe what he wrote how are you going to believe what I say?"

On another Sabbath Jesus was teaching in a synagogue and a woman was there who had been suffering for the past eighteen years with a crippling back problem that left her bent over and unable to straighten herself. This wasn't a purely physical defect as the cause of it was an evil spirit. With his compassion for this woman he asked her to step forward and as everyone watched he said to her, "Woman, you're now set free from your infirmity." He then placed his hands on her and immediately she straightened up and began to praise God.

Because this was the Sabbath the synagogue ruler was furious that Jesus had healed this woman; turning to the rest of the people there he said, "We have six days to do our work, including healing, but the Sabbath isn't for this display of gross violation against the law!"

"You hypocrites!" Jesus shot back at them, "each one of you on the Sabbath releases your ox or donkey from the stall and provides it with water. So why shouldn't this woman, a daughter of Abraham, whom Satan has kept in this condition for eighteen long years, be liberated on the Sabbath day from this severe restriction?"

His critics were stung by this rebuke, but the others were thrilled with all the wonderful things he was doing.[71]

The Pharisees continued to make their attempts at trapping Jesus by catching him out with something he said so that he could be discredited in the eyes of the people. They sent their disciples along

---

[71]   Luke 13:10-17

with the Herodians who would be very interested in his answer to the particular question they had prepared for Jesus. "Teacher," they said with affected respect, "we know that you're a man of integrity and that you teach the way of God truthfully. You're not afraid of being controversial or being intimidated by people of position." After this flattery they got to the question, "Tell us then, what's your opinion on paying taxes – should we pay taxes to Caesar or not?"

Knowing that their intention was to trap him he replied, "You hypocrites, I know what you're trying to do. Bring me a coin that's used for paying the tax." They brought him a denarius,[72] and he asked them, "Whose inscription and portrait is this?"

"Caesar's," they answered.

"Give to Caesar what belongs to him, and to God what is his." When they heard his answer they were impressed and walked away.

The Sadducees, who disagreed with the Pharisees on many things including a belief in the resurrection, presented Jesus with a storyline that was designed to expose an obvious flaw in the resurrection teaching. "Teacher," (the same flattery), "Moses told us that if a man dies without having children, his brother must marry the widow and bear children for him.[73] Now there were seven brothers and the first one married but died without having any children, so his widow married his brother, and then the same thing happened to that brother who died before they could have any children; this happened to the third and fourth right down to the seventh brother and then the woman died. Now the question is: at the resurrection whose wife will she be, as she was married to all seven?"

---

[72] Strict Jews didn't like to handle this coin as it bore a portrait of the emperor.

[73] Deut 25:5-6

"You're making an error," Jesus said to them, "and that's because you don't know the Scriptures or the power of God. At the resurrection there won't be any marriage because they then will be spirit like the angels. But concerning the resurrection itself – the raising of the dead – have you never read what God says to you, 'I am the God of Abraham, the God of Isaac, and the God of Jacob'?[74] He's not the God of the dead but of the living."

When the people heard this they were astonished at his teaching while the Sadducees were silent.

When the Pharisees heard how the Sadducees had failed in their attempt to discredit the belief in the resurrection they some of them congratulated him on getting the better of them, yet they still got together and devised another trick question for him.

One of these teachers of the law, who had heard Jesus debating with the Sadducees, and noted how well Jesus had answered them, asked him, "Of all the commandments, which is the most important?"

"The most important one is this: 'Hear, O Israel, the Lord our God, the Lord is one.[75] Love the Lord your God with all your heart and with all your soul and with all your mind and with all your strength. The second is this: 'Love your neighbour as yourself.'[76]There is no commandment greater than these."

"An answer directly from Scripture, well said, teacher," the lawyer said. "You're right in saying that God is one and there is no other but him and to love him with all that you are and to love your neighbour as yourself is more important than all burnt offerings and sacrifices."

---

[74]   Ex 3:6

[75]   Deut 6:4-5

[76]   Lev 19:18

This wasn't a new concept as Samuel had told Saul "Does the Lord delight in burnt offerings and sacrifices as much as in obeying the voice of the Lord? To obey is better than sacrifice and to heed is better than the fat of rams."[77] Jesus had carefully listened to the question and was aware that an attempt was being made to lead him into saying that the sacrificial system wasn't that important and any statement like that could be taken as speaking against the temple which would be seen by the authorities as treason.

Jesus said to him, "You're not far from the kingdom of God." And from then on no-one dared ask him any more questions.

---

[77]   1 Sam 15:32

Dining with a Pharisee

Jesus had taught his disciples that unless their righteousness surpasses that of the Pharisees and the teachers of the law, they will certainly not enter the kingdom of God. A greater righteousness than theirs is required.

The strongest criticism that Jesus had was for the Pharisees, yet some even from this, the strictest sect in the nation, believed in him, but because they would be expelled from the synagogue if they openly confessed their belief in him they kept silent. Joseph of Arimathea, a member of the Sanhedrin, was a disciple of Jesus, but secretly because he feared the Jews, and Nicodemus, another member of the Sanhedrin, spoke against arresting him saying, "Does our law condemn a man without first hearing him to find out what he is doing?" Because of his protest he was told, "Are you from Galilee too? Look into it, and you'll find that the Prophet doesn't come out of Galilee."[78]

A Pharisee invited Jesus to eat with him and he accepted but when Jesus reclined at the table the Pharisee noticed with surprise that Jesus hadn't first washed before the meal. This washing[79] wasn't out of a concern for personal hygiene but out of the belief that associating with the world, and in particular the Gentiles, left them in an unclean state from which they needed be cleansed. The quantity of water to

---

[78] John 7:50-52

[79] The verb is *baptizŌ*

be used and the details of how it was to be done are found in the Mishnah.

This careful concern over physical washing grieved and angered Jesus who saw all their ceremonial customs as an avoidance of what really mattered, and he became extremely blunt in speaking about their failings.

"You Pharisees clean the outside of your utensils but ignore the insides, which is what your lives are like! On the outside you look righteous but on the inside you're covered in the dirt of your self-righteous hypocrisy! You think that if you're seen fulfilling your religious duties and making a show of giving to the poor and giving long prayers that you'll be clean but the dirt is still there.

"It is with deep regret that I have to tell you that not only have you misrepresented God but you have misled those to whom you are supposed to be an example. You give tithes of your garden herbs but you neglect justice and the love of God – it's not wrong to tithe but you've turned your back on the truly important things concerning where your heart is.

"Your motive in what you do is always to be seen in the best light; you love the most important seats in the synagogue and the respect you get in the market places as you walk around in your flowing robes and to be called 'Rabbi'[80] You make your phylacteries[81] wide and the tassels on your garments long and because some people find it impressive you give long prayers. You're like white-washed tombs, which look beautiful on the outside but inside are full of the bones of the dead and all sorts of filthy things."

---

[80]   Meaning 'teacher' and 'master'

[81]   They were small boxes containing Scripture verses that were worn on the forehead and on the arm.

At this point one of the experts in the law butted in saying, "Teacher, when you say these things you insult us also."

"Too bad for you experts in the law because of the way you load people down with burdens contained in your interpretation of the law and the traditions of the elders; you should have been teaching God's law and inspiring the people, instead you won't even lift a finger to help them, and being a lawyer you know how to get round restrictive regulations particularly concerning the Sabbath.

"You built tombs for the prophets, but it was your forefathers who killed them, and so you advertise that you approve of what your forefathers did. You honour the dead prophets with these splendid tombs but you don't follow what they said. Because of this, God's purpose is to send more prophets and apostles who you will kill and persecute. So this generation will be held responsible for the blood of all the prophets that has been shed since the beginning of the world, from the blood of Abel to the blood of Zechariah[82]who was killed between the altar and the sanctuary. Yes, this generation will be held responsible for it all.

"Disaster is coming to you experts in the law, because you've taken away the key to unlock the knowledge of God so that people can't see the meaning of Scripture which means that you've not been able to enter and you've also made it difficult for others to enter. You've built, through your teachings and traditions, a wall that the people can't get over so that they are unable to see the wonderful things God has for them."

As soon as Jesus left the building the Pharisees and the teachers of the law began to oppose him fiercely and besieging him with questions as they tried to trap him as a hunter going after a wild beast.

---

[82]   See 2 Chron 24:20-22

Collusion with the devil

A demon-possessed man who was also blind and unable to speak was brought to Jesus who healed him so that he could both see and talk. Those who saw this were amazed and shocked; they asked, "Could this really be the Messiah – the Son of David, the One we've been waiting for?"

Hearing these remarks the Pharisees were quick to say that this undeniable miracle was only possible because Beelzebub[83] the prince of demons was behind it.

Jesus knew what they were thinking and said to them, "If a kingdom is at war with itself it'll be ruined, just as a city or household divided against itself will not stand. If Satan is against himself how can his kingdom remain? But if I drive out demons by the prince of demons how do your people do it? On the other hand if what I did was done by the action of God, then you're in the presence of the kingdom of God."

Jesus illustrates what has happened. "If a man enters a strong man's house with the intention of taking his possessions he first has to tie up the strong man before he can take his goods. If you're not with me you're against me, and if you don't gather with me then you're scattering." Then Jesus told them how deadly serious their

---

[83]   May have come from the name of a Canaanite god, Baal-Zebub, 2 Kings 1:2

charge against him was, and what he said then has been distorted and misrepresented to mean something quite different from what he said.

"Every sin and blasphemy will be forgiven, but the blasphemy against the Spirit will not be forgiven, either in this age or the age to come." They had seen at first hand the kindness and power of God at work in taking away a great burden from the man who couldn't see or speak and had a demon within him, and seeing such divine love in action they deliberately attributed it to the prince of demons.

For them there could be no greater display of God's mercy which made their allegation inexcusable. Many since have taken these words and taught that any blasphemy against Jesus can be forgiven, which is true, but have gone on to teach that the Holy Spirit is another person who takes blasphemy far more seriously than Jesus does. The Holy Spirit is God himself, not a part of or a third of God. God is Spirit[84]and what those Pharisees saw was the clear and irrefutable evidence of God's work through the Messiah who was right next to them. They could see and hear him and if they wanted, they could touch him.

Because of what they saw there was no excuse or justification for them to lay such a charge against him, and so their guilt remained. Jesus was later to say to others who were faced with similar evidence that God had done something marvellous. "If you were bind, you wouldn't be guilty of sin; but because you claim that you can see, your guilt remains."[85]

"I tell you that you will have to give an account on the day of judgment for every careless word you've spoken, for by your words you'll be acquitted, and by your words you'll be condemned."

---

[84]   John 4: 24

[85]   John 9: 41

Because of the danger of a partial repentance Jesus gave this story: "When an evil spirit comes out of a person it goes looking for somewhere else to rest and finding nothing suitable it decides to return to the man it was in and when it arrives it finds some improvements have been made but there was still space for him, and others. It finds seven other spirits, worse than itself, and they take up permanent residence in the man so that his condition is more damaged than before; this is how it'll be with this wicked generation."

The apostle Paul wrote of two types of sorrow, but only one that make a real difference: "Even if I caused you sorrow by my letter, I don't regret it; I see that my letter hurt you, but only for a short time, and now I'm happy – not because you were sorry – but because your sorrow led you to repentance. God intended that you become sorrowful and as a result you were not harmed by us. Godly sorrow brings repentance that leads to being saved, and is not to be regretted, but worldly sorrow brings death."[86]

If we pass on a lie unintentionally, the guilt belongs to the one who originated it, not those who had been conned into accepting it as true. Satan, as a master counterfeiter, has lied from the beginning and those lies have resulted in a world full of religions and ideologies that, like an inaccurate map, has led us all in the wrong direction.[87]

---

[86]   2 Cor 7:8-10

[87]   See my 'The Dragon the World and the Christian.'

The Messiah and anxiety

Jesus said to his disciples, "Don't worry about your life, what you're going to eat or what you'll wear. Life is about more that what you eat and wear. God feeds the wild creatures and the birds and you're much more valuable than them. Worrying won't add a single hour to your life – so why do it?

"Look at the flowers and how beautiful they are but even Solomon in all his splendour wasn't clothed like one of these." He picked a flower from the long grass and looking at it said, "This is how God dresses the earth which only lasts a short time and then it's thrown into the fire. How much more will he look after you, who have such little faith. So don't make your physical needs your priority and don't worry about those things – that's what the world is concerned about. Your Father knows that you need to eat and have clothes but your main concern should be looking for the establishment of his kingdom and his righteousness, and all these other things will be given you as well. Don't worry about what's going to happen tomorrow, do what you need to do today."

Jesus was later to tell his disciples, "In this world you will have trouble, but don't worry! I've overcome the world."

Jesus called his followers a small flock[88] but encouraged them not to be afraid because their Father has been pleased to give them the

---

[88]   Luke 12:32

kingdom. "So be awake and ready as you wait for your master to return and when he arrives you'll be able to respond immediately. It'll be good news for those who are found to be awake and watching when he comes, even if there's a long time before he does arrive. Be careful because none of you know exactly when he'll come but I do tell you that it will be at a time when he's not expected."

Peter asked if this information was addressed to them as disciples or to everyone.

"Who is the wise and faithful manager whom the master puts in charge of seeing that his servants are paid at the proper time? When the master returns it'll be good if he finds him carrying out his duties as ordered, and if he is, then that manager will be put in charge of the master's estate. But if the manager thinks that the master will not be back for a long time yet, if at all, and begins to mistreat the master's servants and gets himself repeatedly drunk then the master will come unexpectedly and will cut him to pieces and dumped on the rubbish-tip where all the other unbelievers are.

Many misleadingly say that Jesus came to bring peace and if only enough people believe in him there would be peace throughout the world. This is the opposite of what he taught. "Do you think I came to bring peace on earth? No, my coming will bring division," and then quoting the prophet Micah he goes on to say, "from now on there will be division even in the same family, each person against the other, and a person's enemies will be those of their own household."[89]

"Anyone who is more devoted to his parents or any other family member is not really my disciple, and anyone who isn't prepared to go to their own death as a follower of me is not a true disciple. Whoever has saving their life as their priority will lose it, but whoever loses their life for me will find it."[90]

---

[89]   Micah 7:6

[90]   Matt 10:34-39

The best the world can give is the hope of peace and the wish that someday peace will come. Each New Year's Eve everyone hopes for a better year than the last one, but Jesus gave his disciples real peace and the promise that they would soon experience that quality of mind. On his last night with them he said, "I'm giving you my peace and it's more deep and lasting than the world can give so don't let your minds be troubled and don't be afraid. You heard me when I said that I'm going away and I will come back to you; if you love me you would be glad that I'm going to the Father, because the Father is greater than I am. I've told you this before it happens so that when it does happen you'll believe. I won't speak to you much longer because the prince of this world – Satan, is on his way. He has no hold on me, but the world must learn that I love the Father and that I do exactly what he has commanded me to do."[91]

While Jesus promised his disciples peace no such promise is given to the world. In answer to the question of when that climactic time just prior to his return would happen, and what signs would accompany it, he said, "There will be signs in the sun, moon and stars. On the earth, nations will be in anguish and perplexity at the roaring and tossing of the sea. People will faint for terror, apprehensive of what is coming on the world because even the heavens will be shaken! At that time they will see the Son of Man coming in a cloud with power and great glory. When this happens, stand and lift your head because your liberation is close.

"Be careful, or you'll be weighed down with the cares and anxieties of this life and this day may close on you unexpectedly like a trap, because it will come on everyone who lives on earth – so be on watch, and pray that you may be able to escape all that's going to happen, and to be able to stand before the Son of Man."[92]

---

[91]   John 14:27-31

[92]   Luke 21: 25-36

He also said of that time, "Those will be days of distress unequalled from the beginning when God created the world, until now, and never to be equalled again. If the Lord had not cut short those days, no-one would survive, but for the sake of his chosen people, the elect, he has shortened them. At that time if anyone says to you, 'Look, there's the Messiah!' or 'Look, here he is!' don't believe it because counterfeit Messiahs and false prophets will appear and perform signs and miracles to deceive the elect – if that were possible. Be on your guard; I've told you everything in advance."[93]

The reality of our natural emotions is that we do get anxious and perplexed but the antidote is communicating with the God who makes peace between himself and sinful human beings. Our problems may not be lifted but his promise never to leave us and to grant us eternal life can be trusted.

"Whatever you've learned or received or heard from me, or seen in me" Paul told the Philippians, "put it into practice and the God of peace will be with you."[94]

Jesus experienced anxiety to the level that no other human has. They were on their way up to Jerusalem with Jesus leading the way and the disciples, as well as those who were following, who were sharing their feelings of apprehension and fear because of what may lie ahead of them when he took the twelve to one side and told them clearly what was going to happen to him. "We're going up to Jerusalem and there the Son of Man will be betrayed to the chief priests and teachers of the law. They'll condemn him to death and will hand him over to the Gentiles who will mock him and spit on him, and they'll flog him and then kill him. Three days later he'll rise to life."

---

[93]   Mark 13: 19-23

[94]   Phil 4:9

The disciples didn't understand any of this, because its meaning was hidden from them and they didn't know why he was talking this way, but Jesus knew the rejection and suffering that he was walking towards.

Finally that day came. It was dark and he knew his arrest was imminent. They went to a place called Gethsemane[95]which was a garden on the slopes of the Mount of Olives. Jesus said to his disciples, "Sit here while I pray," and he took Peter and the two brothers, James and John along with him. He began to be deeply distressed and troubled.

"I feel overwhelmed and heartbroken at being so close to death," he said to them, and then he asked them to wait there and keep watch. Walking a short distance further he fell to the ground and prayed, "Abba,[96]as everything is possible for you, take this cup[97]from me so that I don't have to go through this suffering – if there's any other way so that I can avoid this experience then please remove it – yet, if going through with this suffering is the only way to bring reconciliation between you and mankind, then I am committed to your will over what I want."

At that moment an angel appeared to him and gave him strength. Jesus continued to pray and his tension was so great that his sweat was like drops of blood dropping to the ground. He knew what kind of death awaited him and that he was going to become sin itself and take our place and receive the penalty that we deserve. He remembered Isaiah's words, 'Yet it was the Lord's will to crush him and cause him to suffer and though the Lord makes his life a guilt offering...' promises of suffering before glory.

---

[95]   Gethsemane is a transliteration of a Greek word that means 'oil press' or 'oil vat'.

[96]   Aramaic for *Father*

[97]   The 'cup of wrath,' Psa 75:8, Isa 51:17, Jer 25:15, 49:12, Ezek 23:31-34, Rev 14:10, 16:19.

When he got up and went back to his disciples he found them fast asleep. He said to Peter, "Why were you sleeping? Couldn't you stay awake for one hour? Stay awake and pray so that you don't become tempted to deny me – if you don't stay awake and pray you'll fail and then you'll desert me, the spirit is willing but the flesh is weak."

He went away a second time and said to his Father, "If it's not possible for this cup to be taken away unless I drink it, then may your will be done."

When he went back to them they had fallen asleep again and when he woke them they didn't know what to say to him so he left them and went away once more and prayed, saying the same thing.

When he returned for the third time he found them yet again fast asleep. He woke them and said, "That's enough sleep, the time has come for the Son of Man to be handed over into the hands of sinners. Get up and let's go, here comes my betrayer!"

The Messiah and deception

Paul was later able to write to the Thessalonians saying, 'concerning the coming of our Lord Jesus Christ and our meeting him together, we ask you not to become unsettled or alarmed by some prophecy or report or letter that has supposedly come from us, saying that the day of the Lord has already come. Don't let anyone deceive you in any way, because that day will not come until the rebellion that rejects God occurs and the lawless man appears, the man who is destined for destruction.

'He will set himself against everything that is called God or is worshipped and places himself in God's temple, claiming that he is God.[98]

'Don't you remember that when I was with you I used to tell you these things? You know what is holding him back, so that he can appear publicly at the right time. This hidden power of lawlessness has already begun, but the one who restrains it will hold it back and when this control is lifted he will emerge.[99] The Lord will overthrow this lawless one quickly by the splendour of his coming. The lawless

---

[98]   The temple in Jerusalem was destroyed by the Romans in AD 70, could it refer to the church which Paul describes as a temple in which God lives, Eph 2:21-22? It may be unwise to speculate too much apart from saying that this 'lawless man' is human.

[99]   The Thessalonian readers of this letter were in a far better position than us to understand what Paul meant as he had spoken to then before on this subject. For us, it, to some degree, remains an enigma.

one will operate in accord with Satan's power to counterfeit all kinds of miracles and signs and wonders that deceive those who are perishing. The reason they are perishing is that they refused to love the truth and delighted in lawlessness themselves.'

'Whatever happens,' Paul wrote to the Philippians, 'conduct yourselves in a way that's in line with the great news of Christ, so that, whether I come to see you or hear about you I'll know that you stand firm with one mind, contending as one for the belief in the good news without fearing in any way those who oppose you. This is evidence that they will be destroyed and you will be saved.' Then Paul makes it clear that although their positive attitude is one of peace there is no immunity from the sufferings that others go through, 'It has been granted to you on behalf of Christ not only to believe on him, but also to suffer for him, since you're going through the same struggle you saw I had, and now hear that I still have.'

The four horsemen of Revelation[100] are led by a rider that is identified by many as Christ riding out on a white horse to conquer; yet following that rider is war, starvation and death, which taken together, reveal the first rider in a different light. These images, like everything else in the book of Revelation, are highly symbolic, and are representations of the prevailing conditions that have always been with us and will remain until Christ returns. The first rider is a figurative illustration of a counterfeit Messiah making converts by force, and not by faith as God calls people to believe.

This fits in neatly with the answer Jesus gave his disciples when he was asked what is going to happen in the world before his coming in glory to inaugurate the new age.[101] They were sitting on the Mount of Olives looking across the Kidron Valley to Herod's temple which was built in the best of Greco-Roman architecture for that time. The

---

[100]   Rev 6:1-2

[101]   Matt 24, Mk 13, Luke 21.

white stone facades were topped off in parts with gold which made it dazzling to gaze at when the rising sun hit it. The work on the temple was still not finished and scaffolding could be seen around its sides.

The disciples were drawing the attention of Jesus to the huge foundational stones that the temple rested on and the magnificence of the buildings when he interrupted their enthusiasm by stating, "What you're admiring so much is all going to be destroyed – every stone is going to be thrown down."

"Tell us then," the disciples asked, "when will this happen and what will be the sign of your coming?"

Jesus went on to speak of wars and rumours of wars, nation against nation, famines and earthquakes in different areas, and not to be alarmed because these are just the beginnings of what he called 'birth pangs', but the first thing he spoke of was to "watch out that no-one deceives you, because many will come in my name claiming that I am the Saviour, but they'll deceive many, and many false prophets will appear and they also will deceive many. Like the first rider in Revelation the Christ that will be taught and imposed on the world is a counterfeit, and not the real Jesus of the Bible who taught that "My kingdom is not of this age – if it were, my servants would fight to prevent my arrest by the Jews – but my kingdom belongs to another age."[102]

Over the many centuries since Jesus said these words many leaders have gone to war claiming to be a defender of the faith and to represent the Christ, and in his name have put to death all who disagreed with their rule and what they ordered to be accepted as the truth. The church authorities have used the state to persecute and imposed the death penalty on those they designated as heretics. Freedom of choice over a person's belief was nonexistent.

---

[102]   John 18:36

These deceptions began very early in church history. Paul said to the leaders of the Ephesian church, "I know that after I leave savage wolves will enter among you and will not spare the flock. Even from your own number there will be men who distort the truth in order to draw away disciples to themselves. So be on your guard! Remember that for the past three years I've never stopped warning you night and day with tears."[103]

He wrote to Timothy, 'In the presence of God and of Christ Jesus, who will judge the living and the dead, and in mind of his appearing and his kingdom, I'm giving you this duty of care: Preach the Word; be prepared whatever the time; correct, rebuke and encourage, with patience and careful instruction. For the time will come when men will not put up with sound teaching. Instead, to suit their own desires, they will attach themselves to a great number of teachers who will say what they really want to hear, and their ears will turn from the truth to myths. But you, keep control of yourself in all situations, endure hard times, do the work of a bearer of the good news and discharge all the duties of the vocation you've been called to.'[104]

Jesus had given the reason to his disciples why his followers would suffer at the hands of those who, in their blindness, considered themselves as faithful followers of Christ: "They will put you out of the synagogue, in fact, a time is coming when anyone who kills you will think he's offering a service to God. They'll do these things because they don't know the Father or me. I've told you this so that when the time comes you'll remember that I warned you. I didn't tell you before because I was still with you."[105]

The warnings of persecution and the distortion of the message are fully recorded in the pages of history with the deep divisions within

---

[103]   Acts 20:29-31

[104]   2 Tim 4:1-5

[105]   This was said on his last night with his disciples. John 16:2-4

Christianity plain for all to see. Each denomination could stake their claim of greater faithfulness to the teaching of Christ above those who some might consider as their brothers and sisters in the faith. As Jonathan Wright has said in his book 'Heretics,' 'Sectarian hatred (let alone well-mannered antagonism) is still with us.'

For many the criterion for distinguishing between a true Christian and a false one is whether they subscribe to one or more of the creeds formulated by the early church fathers in the fourth century; yet many of these church elders were strongly influenced by Platonism.[106] For them the creeds form a non-negotiable base line for orthodoxy which if a person rejects he or she then faces the certainty of being labelled as siding with one of the heretical groups. But the so-called heretical groups would see themselves as the defenders of the true faith while, in many cases, they too share distortions just as serious as those they charge with serious theological errors.

Some see Athanasius as the great defender of the true faith and Arius, the villain of the Arian controversy, and yet Athanasius was guilty of using violence against those who disagreed with him. Augustine of Hippo also employed the state forces to punish those who, in his reasoning, had crossed the correct theological line. Calvin was not against capital punishment for those who would deny what he considered foundational to Christian teaching. Luther, who hated the Anabaptists (they believed in a separation of church and state; that the soul is mortal and that the lost are destroyed forever in the lake of fire), said of them, 'who cannot see here in the Anabaptists, not men possessed by demons, but demons themselves possessed by worse demons?'[107]

To be fair to these unorthodox groups, who are just as sincere and devoted as those who are mainly considered orthodox, adding to and

---

[106]   See Ivor J. Davidson's 'The Birth of the Church' page 30.

[107]   Luther's preface to his commentary of the letter to the Galatians

distorting the Scriptures is exactly what the mainstream churches have done, which is seen when they claim that the creeds are necessary for a better and clearer understanding of Christian theology, even though they came centuries after the Scriptures were completed. All fellowships, without exception, have either taken away or added to Scripture and in that toxic procedure have misrepresented what Jesus actually said and mislead millions in what Jesus intends for the future of this world, and the destiny of its inhabitants.

Satan had gone from deceiving the first woman to deceiving the whole world.[108]It's not that when a person becomes a Christian they're no longer deceived, because whatever denomination we enter, we inherit a set of teachings that were established long ago and these distinctive teachings then become our beliefs, which are gratefully accepted as true as we happily join our new spiritual family, yet those beliefs may be very different from others who, just as sincerely, worship perhaps a short distance away, but remain strangers to us, because their distinctive beliefs put themselves outside of our fellowship. Yet God in his wisdom has people in all denominations and even outside of a fellowship that are known to him because they belong to him and all of them form the one spiritual body sharing the same Father and the same Lord.

In Jesus' prayer, spoken on the night of his last meal, he said, "My prayer isn't for them alone. I pray also for those who will believe in me through their message, that all of them might be one."[109]

Paul wrote, 'I appeal to you, brothers, in the name of our Lord Jesus Christ, that all of you agree with one another so that there may be no divisions among you and that you may be perfectly united in mind and thought.'[110]The fact was that there were divisions among

---

[108]   Gen 3: 1, 4. Rev 12:9

[109]   John 17:20-21

[110]   1 Cor 1:10

them and Paul needed to address those failings. Divisions are normal in this world, whether in the church or out of it. These differences and hostility between both secular and religious people will not be overcome as long as the unseen ruler of this world is still in control. Those who are in Christ should no longer hold on to any hostility towards anyone believing differently to them but recognise that God has his people in every fellowship and outside of any established group; their unity is a spiritual one and is not dependant on which denomination you attend or even if you're not attending a particular fellowship.

"What do you think?" Jesus asked the leading priests and the elders of the people, "There was a man who had two sons and he went to the first and said, 'Son, go and work in the vineyard.'

'I won't,' he answered, but later he changed his mind and went.

Then the father went to the other son and said the same thing, 'I will sir,' but he didn't go.'

"Which of the two did what his father wanted?"

"The first," they answered.

"I'm telling you the truth," Jesus said to them, "the hated tax collectors and the despised prostitutes are entering the kingdom of God before you, because John the Baptist came to show you the way of righteousness, and you didn't believe him, but the tax collectors and the prostitutes did, and even after you saw this you didn't repent and believe him."

It is perhaps the most unlikely to whom God grants repentance and faith, while those who hold high positions in the church and are regarded as being closer to God may be the last and not the first.

This worldwide religious deception that has impacted all of us without exception will only be taken away when the deceiver – the father of lies – is made inactive and will no longer be allowed to influence humans. This great act of liberation only comes with the return of the King who refused to submit to Satan's suggestions and schemes.[111]

"Submit yourselves, to God. Resist the devil, and he'll go from you. Come near to God and he'll come near to you."[112]

"Be self-controlled and alert. Your enemy the devil prowls around like a roaring lion looking for someone to eat. Resist him, standing firm in the faith, because you know that your brothers throughout the world are undergoing the same kind of sufferings."[113]

In the highly symbolic writing contained in the book of Revelation there is a description of an event at the birth of Jesus that is rarely portrayed in paintings and films. It begins with a woman clothed with the sun, with the moon under her feet and a crown of twelve stars on her head; this, like all the other images in Revelation, pointed back to Scripture; in this case, Joseph's dream that looked forward to the time when he would save the family of Israel because of his high position in Egypt.[114]

But now the picture changes from the promise of salvation to a woman in pain because she was about to give birth, but unseen to anyone there an enormous red dragon stood in front of the woman so that it could destroy her child the moment it was born. The child survived; it was a boy who will rule the nations with an iron sceptre. This takes us back to the second Psalm where we read, 'He said to

---

[111]   Rev 20:1-3

[112]   James 3:7

[113]   1 Peter 5:8-9

[114]   Gen 37:9

me, "you are my Son; today I have become your Father. Ask of me, and I will make the nations your inheritance, the ends of the earth your possession. You will rule them with an iron sceptre; you will dash them to pieces like pottery." This referred to the great King David but also pointed forward to a greater king who would rule over all nations. "Today in the town of David a Saviour has been born to you; he is the Messiah – the Lord"[115]

Isaiah had written of a future golden reign, 'For to us a child is born, to us a son is given, and the government will be on his shoulders. And he will be called Wonderful Counsellor, Mighty God, Everlasting Father, Prince of Peace. Of the increase of his government and peace there will be no end. He will reign on David's throne and over his kingdom, establishing and upholding it with justice and righteousness from that time on and forever.'[116]

When Isaiah wrote this, David had been dead for the past 230 years and so there was another David to come; a king who would rule as God over Israel, restoring its former greatness and extending his rule over all other nations.

Jeremiah was also to write, "The days are coming," declares the Lord, "when I will raise up to David a righteous Branch, a king who will reign wisely and do what is right and just in the land. In his days Judah will be saved and Israel will live in safety. This is the name by which he will be called: The Lord Our Righteousness."[117] Jeremiah later wrote, "They will serve the Lord their God and David their king whom I will raise up for them."[118] Ezekiel, writing about the same time, has, "I will place over them one shepherd, my servant David."[119]

---

[115]   Luke 2:11

[116]   Isa 9:6-7

[117]   Jer 23:5-6

[118]   Jer 30:9

[119]   Ezek 34:23

Both from the prophets and the hope of the people was for a descendent of David to come and liberate the nation from foreign rule. Paul wrote to the Roman Christians and at the beginning of his letter said, "Paul, a servant of Jesus Christ, called to be an apostle and set apart for the gospel of God – the gospel he promised before through his prophets in the Holy Scriptures regarding his Son, who as to his human nature was a descendent of David."

Jesus was speaking to the teachers of the law when he said, "How is it that they say the Messiah is the son of David and yet David himself writes in the Psalms: 'The Lord said to my Lord. "Sit at my right hand until I put your enemies under your feet.'[120]If David calls him 'Lord' how can he be his son?"

No-one was able to reply to his question.

The expectation was that a king just like David or even greater would come and restore the nation to its former glory, but although Jesus was descended from the lineage of David he was in fact David's Lord with an authority that extends much further than any of them listening to him could have imagined.

Before the ruling body of Israel – the Sanhedrin, the high priest stood up and looking with contempt at the abandoned helpless prisoner before him asked, his words full of anger, "I charge you under oath by the living God: Tell us if you are the Messiah, the Son of God."

"Yes," Jesus confidently answered the high priest, and then addressing all of them there he said, "In the future you will see the Son of Man sitting at the right hand of the Mighty One and coming on the clouds of heaven."

---

[120]   Psa 110:1

Not only did Jesus refer back to that same psalm of David when he spoke of sitting at God's right hand, he directly quoted from Daniel's vision where he said, "In my vision at night I saw one like a son of man, coming with the clouds of heaven. He approached the Ancient of Days and was led into his presence and he was given authority, glory and sovereign power. All people of every language worshipped him and his kingdom is an everlasting kingdom that will never end or be destroyed."[121]

Jesus had already told his disciples concerning his return that "the sun will be darkened and the moon will not give its light; the stars will fall from the sky and the heavenly bodies will be shaken.[122] At that time the sign of the Son of man will appear in the sky and all the nations will mourn as they see the Son of man coming on the clouds with power and great glory."

"Blasphemy!" shouted the high priest as he tore at his clothes, "we don't need any more witnesses – you've heard him for yourselves; what do you think?" They all as one responded, "He's worthy of death."

Then they, which included the guards, spat in his face and hit him with their fists. Others, after they had blindfolded him, slapped him while cruelly demanding that he answer to the question, "who hit you?"

Many centuries earlier Isaiah had written, 'I offered my back to those who beat me, my cheeks to those who pulled out my beard; I didn't hide my face from mocking and spitting.'[123]

Jesus had taught his followers that they shouldn't resist an evil person and to give them no resistance. If you are treated with contempt

---

[121]   Dan 7:13

[122]   Isa 13:10

[123]   Isa 50:6

and insulted, don't fight back, accept it as Christ's servant and as he did himself – submitting himself to his Father. The Christian's response to evil must not conform to the way the world responds.

Paul, in writing to the Romans, said 'Don't repay anyone evil for evil. Be careful to do what's right, and if it's possible, as far as you're concerned, live at peace with everyone. Don't take revenge, but leave room for God's wrath, because it's written, "It's mine to avenge; I'll repay."[124]On the contrary: "If your enemy is hungry, feed him; if he's thirsty, give him something to drink. In doing this, you'll be heaping burning coals on his head."[125]Don't be overcome by evil, but overcome evil with good.'

---

[124]   Deut 32:35

[125]   Prov 25:21-22

Talking to God

Part 1

"When you pray," Jesus said to his disciples when one of them, after seeing him pray, asked, "Lord, teach us to pray, just as John taught his disciples." Jesus went on to give them a prayer that could be used corporately or as the basis of a private prayer. His emphasis was to keep it simple and preferably short.

"Our Father[126]in heaven, holy is your name, your kingdom come, your will be done on earth as it is in heaven. Give us today our daily bread. Forgive us the debt we owe you, as we also have forgiven those who owe anything to us, and keep us clear of temptation, and save us from the evil one."

What is repeated many times over can easily lose its focus and emphasis. After addressing God as our Father the first priority in life is the seeking of God's kingdom, which Jesus announced is near, and his command to repent was given as a matter of great urgency.

Paul wrote that God has rescued us from the dominion of darkness and brought us into the kingdom of the Son he loves.[127]But even though Christians are citizens of that kingdom now, they live in this world like ambassadors waiting for his return. 'When Christ, who is

---

[126]   In Aramaic it is *abba*.

[127]   Col 1:13, 3:4

your life, appears, then you also will appear with him in glory.' While this is an evil age[128]we're to pray for his return and begin his reign until all his enemies are under his feet.[129]Jesus used the expression, 'the people of this age,' in the sense of belonging to this world but of those who belong to the Messiah, he said, "the world has hated them because they are not of the world any more than I am of the world... as you [the Father] sent me into the world so I've sent them into the world."[130]

The good news is that the kingdom of God is coming. Not by the growth and spread of Christianity, which is divided and splintered into thousands of diverse groups and has a history of violence and persecution that more reflects this world and this age rather than the age to come.

What Jesus promised that will happen is that "this gospel of the kingdom will be preached in the whole world as a testimony to all nations, and then the end will come."[131] Not the end of the world, but the beginning of a wonderful and glorious new age of real peace free from disasters and corruption. It's inescapable and unavoidable, and each day brings that liberation closer.

That preaching of the coming kingdom will neither convince nor convert the majority of the world's populations but is given as an announcement to the world that this age is coming to an end.

---

[128]   Gal 1:4

[129]   1 Cor 15:25

[130]   John 17:14,18.

[131]   Matt 24:14

Your will be done on earth

Part 2

Heaven exists; it is a place, or is it much more than a place? Heaven is where glory and splendour transcend any human attempts at adequately describing it. Jesus said to his disciples on his last night with them, "You heard me say, 'I'm going away and I'm coming back to you.' If you loved me, you would be glad that I'm going to the Father, because the Father is greater than I."[132]

The writer of the letter to the Hebrews wrote, 'Let us fix our eyes on Jesus, the author and the one who brings our faith to completion, who for the joy set before him endured the cross, scorning its shame, and sat down at the right hand of the throne of God.'[133]That joy in the light of God is beyond human language but God condescends to our weakness in giving us comparisons with the earthly and the heavenly to ignite our imagination. Our weakness will, at the resurrection, be replaced with power, our mortality will be clothed with immortality, our limitations will be changed to being indestructible and our sinful nature will be a thing of the past.

Life in this world is the opposite. Here we live with pain and damage; lives cut off prematurely, injustice and cruelty, poverty and waste. Jesus, as the Son of God, came into the world, and though

---

[132]   John 14:28

[133]   Heb 12:2

the world was made through him it didn't recognise him. With his coming, light had come into the world and near the end of his life he said to his disciples, "You're going to have the light just a little while longer. Walk while you have the light, before darkness overtakes you. The man who walks in the dark doesn't know where he's going. Put your trust in the light while you have it, so that you may become sons of light."[134]

Except for the work God is doing in this world there is no light in it. When Jesus was arrested he said to those there, "Am I leading a rebellion, and is that why you have clubs and swords? Every day I was with you in the temple courts, and you didn't lay a hand on me, but this is your hour – when darkness reigns."[135]

Jesus was referring to more than the fact that it was night-time. Spiritual darkness reigns in this world just as sin reigns in death.[136] Yet even in the darkness God's will is being done; in turning individual lives from darkness to light, and from the power of Satan to God.[137]

When Jesus asked his disciples to pray that God's will be done on earth as it is in heaven, that petition pointed to more than his people enduring patiently in a world they didn't belong to but to a time yet in the future when all that is on the earth will be completely compatible with what is in heaven; a unity between both that will reflect its harmony and oneness.

Paul spoke of this as formally being a mystery that had not up to that time been revealed. He wrote to the Ephesians saying, 'And God has made known to us the mystery of his will according to his good pleasure, which he purposed in Christ, to be put into effect when the

---

134   John 12:35-36

135   Luke 22:52-53

136   Rom 5:21

137   Acts 26:18

times will have reached their fulfilment – to bring all things in heaven and on earth together under one head, even Christ.'[138]

It was never intended that the church would grow to the point where it would dominate and control this world – it was always to be a minority; unrecognised and living as aliens in the world. Jesus said to them, "Don't be afraid, little flock, for your Father has been pleased to give you the kingdom."[139]

Our daily prayer is for God's kingdom to come and that eventually in Christ's reign there will be complete harmony between heaven and earth. This great promise has been supplanted by the lie of going to heaven and leaving this earth to whatever its fate will be. This is far from what Scripture teaches us about the destiny of the earth. Jesus spoke of inheriting the kingdom of God or of inheriting everlasting life, but he never said that his people would go to heaven.

During the second world war the occupied nations of Europe waited in hope for their liberation, while in ancient Egypt, in the time of Moses, a slave people had no idea that they would be liberated from the tyranny that ruled over them. Sometime in the future not just one nation, like ancient Israel or even a group of nations, as Europe under Nazism, will compare with the liberation of the whole world when it comes. No one knows the joy of liberation except those who have experienced it. Paul wrote to the Galatians saying, 'Scripture declares that the whole world is a prisoner of sin.'[140]Whether directly or indirectly we all experience the effects of sin: our own and that of others. Christians, who have been liberated through faith in the Messiah, are encouraged to throw off everything that hinders and

---

[138]   Eph 1:9-10

[139]   Luke 12:32

[140]   Gal 3:22

the sin that so easily entangles, and run with perseverance the race marked out for them.[141]

'I urge you,' Paul writes to the Christians in Rome, 'in view of God's mercy, to offer your bodies as living sacrifices, holy and pleasing to God. This is your spiritual act of worship. Don't conform any longer to how things are done in this world but be changed by the renewing of your mind – then you'll be able to test and approve what God's will is – his good, pleasing and perfect will.[142]

To the Thessalonians he wrote, 'It's God's will that you should be sanctified:[143]that you should avoid sexual immorality and that each of you should learn to control your own body in a way that's holy and honourable.' And later he added, 'Be always joyful; pray always; be thankful in all circumstances, for this is God's will for you in the Messiah Jesus.'

---

[141]   Heb 12:1

[142]   Rom 12:1-2

[143]   Sanctification is the state of being made holy which God does in his people.

Our daily needs

Part 3

"Give us today our daily bread" is for many of us in our modern industrialised countries difficult to relate to because bread in all its varieties is always available in our shops and supermarkets. We're spoilt for choice; each has their favourite bread and there's always plenty more to taste. Daily bread is an expression to cover food in general but also in this context is taken to imply all of our basic needs which Jesus said that God knows we need,[144] as well as knowing those things that we're anxious about. God cares for his people.

There is a section of the book of Proverbs where Agur says, "give me neither poverty nor riches, but give me only my daily bread, otherwise I may have too much and disown you and say, 'Who's the lord?' or I may become poor and steal, and so dishonour the name of my God."[145]

'Today' is a very important word that reoccurs in both the Old Testament and the New Testament. Behind it is the urgent necessity of doing the right thing now, while you still can. In regard to prayer that word 'today' teaches us that speaking to God is a daily occurrence in mind, heart and in words.

---

[144]   Matt 6:32, 1 Peter 5:6-7

[145]   Prov 30:8-9

"Today, if you hear his voice, don't harden your hearts."[146] So many people say, "I'll do it later," which can lead to disaster, because none of us know how long we have. The writer of the letter to the Hebrews says, 'encourage one another daily, as long as it's called 'Today', so that none of you become hardened by sin's deceitfulness.'[147] Our needs come daily and they need to be accompanied by our daily prayers.

---

[146]   Heb 4:7, Psa 95:7-8

[147]   Heb 3:13

Forgiveness

Part 4

"Forgive us our debts just as we have forgiven our debtors." Jesus went on to say, "If you forgive those who sin against you, your heavenly Father will also forgive you, but if you don't forgive others their sins, your Father will not forgive your sins." Paul wrote to the Colossians saying, 'Bear with each other and forgive whatever grievances you may have against one another. Forgive just as the Lord forgave you.'

Jesus said to his disciples, "Things that cause people to sin are bound to come, but disaster will come to the person who causes it. It would be better for that person to be thrown into the sea with a huge weight tied round their neck than to cause one that believes in me to sin, so keep a check on yourselves.

"If your brother sins, rebuke him, and if he repents, forgive him. If he sins against you seven times a day, and seven times comes back to you and says, 'I repent,' forgive him."

Repentance comes before forgiveness as Peter told those who had gathered to hear him on the day of Pentecost. "Repent and be baptised, every one of you, in the name of Jesus the Messiah for the forgiveness of your sins." On a later occasion he said, "Repent and turn to God, so that your sins may be wiped out."[148]

---

[148]   Acts 2:38, 3:19.

Jesus was at dinner, having been invited by a Pharisee, when a woman who had a reputation for a sinful life in that town stood behind him weeping. She had been told he was there and so she brought an alabaster jar of costly perfume to the house. Jesus was reclining on his side having taken his sandals off. She kneeled at his feet and her tears dropped onto his bare feet and she wiped them with her hair as though it was just the two of them there. She kissed his feet and poured the perfume on them.

The Pharisee was shocked by what she was doing and said within himself, 'If he were a real prophet he'd know what sort of sinner this woman is.' Jesus looked towards his host; "Simon, I've something to tell you."

"Go ahead, teacher."

"Two men owed money to a money lender. One owed him the equivalent of close to two year's wages, the other one just two month's wages. The problem was that they both had nothing to pay the debt off with. Strangely, both of their debts were cancelled. Which one of them do you think would appreciate that cancelation the most?"

"I suppose the one who had the larger debt cancelled," Simon replied.

"You're right," Jesus said.

While looking at the woman Jesus said to Simon, "Look at this woman; I entered your house and you didn't give me any water for my feet, but she wet my feet with her tears and wiped them with her hair. You didn't give me a kiss, but this woman hasn't stopped kissing my feet. You didn't put oil on my head, but she has poured perfume on my feet. Her many sins have been forgiven because she appreciates so much what has been done for her. But the person who hasn't experienced that complete forgiveness can't show that depth of appreciation."

Jesus said to her, "Your sins are forgiven."

The other guests were astonished at what they saw as blasphemy. Jesus ignored their stony looks and said to the woman, "Your faith has saved you; the peace of God will go with you."

In one of the stories Jesus gave to teach his disciples about forgiveness he said, "A king wanted to settle accounts with his servants and as he began to do this a man who owed him what amounted to a billion pounds was brought to him. There was no way he could pay it so the master ordered that he and his wife and children and everything he had to be sold to go towards repaying the debt.

"The servant fell to his knees and begged the master to be patient with him and that he would pay everything back. The servant's master had pity on him and cancelled the debt and let him go.

"When that servant left he found a fellow servant of his who owed him just a few pounds. He grabbed him by the neck and demanded that he pay back what owed him. He fell in front of him and begged for patience and that he would pay it all back.

"His desperate plea was refused, and the servant ordered that the man be thrown into prison until he could raise the money. When the other servants saw what had happened they were deeply upset and told their master about it.

"The master had that servant brought before him and said to him, 'You wicked servant – I cancelled that huge debt of yours because you begged me to. Shouldn't you have shown the same mercy on that other servant as I did for you?' The master in his anger handed him over to the torturers until he was able to pay back what he owed.

"This is how my heavenly Father will treat each of you unless you forgive your brother from your heart."

Jesus had earlier said, "If you don't want to be judged then don't judge; if you don't want to be condemned then don't condemn, and if you want to be forgiven, then you forgive."

It was about nine in the morning when the execution began. The three condemned men had reached the area near to the Damascus gate, chosen for executions because of the volume of people that would be using that entry and exit point and would not be able to avoid seeing what was being done there. Executions always drew a huge crowd. The three condemned men were stripped naked and their clothes put to one side. Public disgrace was part of the punishment. As the growing mass of people eagerly and impatiently waited for this grisly display of a slow death to begin they enjoyed themselves by mocking and shouting insults at the one known as the false messiah. He was once seen as possibly their liberator but many were disappointed by his lack of direct action against the Roman authorities and now he was seen as a pretender and a liar who deserved what was coming to him. Circulating around the noisy crowd vendors were doing well with assorted drinks and unleavened cakes.

The nails were fastened by Roman auxiliaries through the prisoner's wrists to the crossbeam that each condemned man had been forced to carry, and once securely attached it was lifted onto a bare tree trunk stained many times over with blood and bodily waste that the agony of dying had caused to be loosened. The stumps of a few branches remained to serve as places to secure the crossbeam. These stunted killing trees were permanently fixed in full visibility for all executions held near to the city gate. The feet of the condemned men were nailed close to the base of the tree and while this was happening Jesus began to repeat the words, "Father, forgive them, because they don't realise what they're doing."

They were to hang there for the next six hours.

Temptation and the evil one

Part 5

Jesus was tempted by the devil to avoid all the discomfort, rejection and pain he knew he would face, and being human and physically vulnerable there would be a natural desire to be comfortable, safe and perhaps even respected, which would be an attractive alternative to persecution and a long and painful death. The devil was doing the tempting but God was doing the testing and Jesus proved in that testing his love through obedience to his Father. Unlike the nation of Israel, whose history is well documented in the Scriptures as one of rebellion against the God who led them out of slavery and into the land that was promised to their forefathers, Abraham, Isaac and Jacob.

The author of the letter to the Hebrews says that 'although he was a son, he learned obedience from what he suffered and once made perfect, he became the source of eternal salvation for all who obey him.'[149]One of the titles of Jesus is High Priest, and so we read, "Therefore, since we have a great high priest who has returned into God's realm, Jesus the Son of God, let's hold firmly to the faith we claim is true, because we don't have a high priest who is unable to identify with our weaknesses, but we have one who has been tempted in every way, just as we are – yet without sin. Let's approach the throne of grace with confidence, so that we may receive mercy and find grace to help us in our time of need."

---

[149]   Heb 5:8. Heb 4:14-16

It is with the thought of our very real vulnerability and weakness that the last part of the prayer that Jesus gave, as a guide for his disciples, addresses the reality of our enemy, the devil. Although some Christians don't believe the devil as a real being exists, Jesus did, and demons often recognised who he was when he was commanding them to leave some unfortunate person who had one or more of these evil spirits within them. On one occasion, a man who was possessed by an evil spirit cried out, "What do you want with us, Jesus of Nazareth? Have you come to destroy us? I know who you are – the Holy One of God!"

Jesus spoke sternly to the spirit, "Be quiet! Come out of him!" The man shook and shrieked as the evil spirit left him.[150]

The prayer that Jesus gave his followers is a plea not to succumb to temptation because we are weak and can easily give in and it is a request for God, whose aim is to build up his people, not to allow the temptation because Satan's aim is to destroy God's people – this he will not be able to do – but he has been successful in misleading many Christians through the acceptance of philosophical ideas that was considered by the early Roman church as wisdom and became part of orthodox teaching. Such teaching, as the immortality of the soul and that of eternal suffering for the lost come from writings outside of Scripture yet are now taken as sound biblical teaching.

As well as providing this framework of prayer, he also warned against the type of prayer that all of them had probably heard from the religious leaders. "When you pray don't be like the hypocrites, because they love to pray standing in the synagogues and on the street corners to be seen by men. I'm telling you the truth; they've received their reward in full. But when you pray, go into your room, close the door and pray to your Father, who is unseen – then your Father, who sees what is done in secret, will reward you.

---

[150]   Mark 1:23-26

"And when you pray don't keep on and on like the pagans, because they think they'll be more effective if they give long prayers. Don't copy them! Because your Father knows what you need before you ask him."[151]

Jesus taught his disciples that they should always pray and not give up. He gave some stories to illustrate this, "There was a judge who didn't fear God and wasn't that interested in people's problems, but this particular widow repeatedly came to him wanting justice against her adversary. He resisted her urgent requests for a while but he got to the point when he was getting worn out by her continuing to bother him. So, to get rid of her he saw to it that she got what she needed even though he still didn't really care one way or the other.

"The unjust judge finally gave the widow justice, but how much more will God bring justice for his chosen ones who cry to him day and night? Will he be indifferent to their prayers? No, He'll see that justice is done, and when it happens it'll be done quickly, but when the Son of Man comes, will he find faith on the earth?"

He then gave an account of two people who went to the temple to pray, "One was a Pharisee and the other a tax collector. The Pharisee stood up and focusing on what he did, said, 'God, I thank you that I'm not like other men – thieves, evildoers, adulterers – or even like this tax collector. I fast twice a week and give a tenth of all I get.'

"The tax collector stood at a distance with his head bowed and beating his chest simply said, 'God, have mercy on me, a sinner.'

"This man, not the Pharisee, went home justified before God, because everyone who praises himself will be humbled, but the person who humbles himself will be praised."

---

[151]   Matt 6:5-8

Later, Peter was to be told by Jesus that he would deny knowing him and that all the disciples would be scattered as the unseen ruler of this world, Satan, wanted to disrupt them emotionally and disable them from being faithful. Jesus said to Peter and included the other disciples as well, "Simon, Simon, Satan has asked to shake you to your core, but I've prayed for you that your failure of nerve will not be permanent and when you've been restored, strengthen your brothers."[152]

The Prayer Jesus gave his disciples teaches that Christians are to address the One Holy God as Father and to pray for his kingdom to come so that eventually the earth and heaven can be one. Prayer is to be made for our daily needs, and forgiveness must be given as well as received. Pray for strength and encouragement in going through trials and for protection from Satan.

---

[152]   Luke 22:31-32

The Reward

Isaiah placed the reward for God's people at the time of his coming in power, "You, who bring good news to Zion, go up on a high mountain. You who bring good news to Jerusalem, lift up your voice with a shout, lift it up and don't be afraid; say to the towns of Judah, "Here is your God!" See, the Sovereign Lord comes with power, and his arm rules for him. See, his reward is with him, and his recompense accompanies him."[153]

The book of Revelation picks up the same message, "Look! I am coming soon. My reward is with me, and I'll give to everyone according to what they've done."[154]

Addressing his disciples Jesus said, "Blessed are the poor in spirit, for theirs is the kingdom of heaven. Blessed are those who mourn, for they will be comforted. Blessed are the meek, for they will inherit the earth. Blessed are those who hunger and thirst for righteousness, for they will be filled. Blessed are the merciful, for they will be shown mercy. Blessed are the pure in heart, for they will see God. Blessed are the peacemakers, for they will be called sons of God. Blessed are those who are persecuted because of righteousness, for theirs is the kingdom of heaven. Blessed are you when people insult you, persecute you and falsely say all kinds of evil against you because of me.

---

[153]   Isa 40:9-10, repeated in 62:11.

[154]   Rev 22:12

"Rejoice and be glad, because great is your reward in heaven, for in the same way they persecuted the prophets who were before you."[155]

Although the Christians' reward is in heaven it will only be given when the Saviour returns to earth because he brings that reward with him. Paul, writing to the Philippians, says, 'Our citizenship is in heaven, and we eagerly wait for a Saviour from there, the Lord Jesus Christ, who, by the power that enables him to bring everything under his control, will transform our human bodies so that they'll be like his glorious body.'[156]

Paul wrote to Timothy, 'I've fought the good fight, I've finished the race, I've kept the faith. Now there is in store for me the crown of righteousness, which the Lord, the righteous Judge, will award me on that day – and not only me, but also to all who have longed for his appearing.'[157]

Peter says something very similar to what Paul had written, 'When the Chief Shepherd appears, you'll receive the crown of glory that will never fade away.'[158] He had previously written that the Christian's imperishable inheritance is kept in heaven.

The promise of reward is always tied to the return of the King, never to the Christian going to heaven to receive it, although many will insist it does. To the Colossians Paul wrote, 'When Christ, who is your life, appears, then you also will appear with him in glory.'[159] And to the Thessalonians he writes, 'May he strengthen your hearts

---

[155]   Matt 5:3-12

[156]   Phil 3:20-21

[157]   2 Tim 4:7-8

[158]   1 Peter 5:4, 1:4

[159]   Col 3:4, 1 Thes 3:13

so that you will be blameless and holy in the presence of our God and Father when our Lord Jesus Christ comes with all his holy ones.'

It is when Christ appears at his return that we will be with him.

As to when the Messiah returns, many individuals and groups have fallen into all sorts of problems by claiming to know the date and have deliberately ignored what Jesus himself said: "No-one knows about that day or hour, not even the angels in heaven, nor the Son, but only the Father." He then goes on to make a comparison between the great flood of Noah's time and his return. "As it was in the days of Noah, so it'll be at the coming of the Son of Man because before the flood people were living normally right up to the day when Noah entered the ark, and they knew nothing about what would happen until the flood came and took them all away.

"That is how it will be at the coming of the Son of Man." Jesus then goes on to emphasise the importance of constant readiness and the very real division between people. "Two men will be in the field; one will be taken and the other left. Two women will be grinding with a hand mill (or in the same supermarket!); one will be taken and the other left.

"So keep watch, because you don't know on what day your Lord will come, but understand this: If the owner of the house knew what time of night the thief was coming, he would have kept watch and wouldn't have allowed his house to be broken into. So you must be ready because the Son of Man will come at a time when you don't expect him.[160]

"With these things in mind, who is the faithful and wise servant who has been put in charge during his master's absence? It'll be good for that servant if when his master returns he's found to be taking good care of what he has been entrusted with. Because of his

---

[160]   See 1 Thes 5:1-6

faithfulness to his master he'll be richly rewarded. But if that servant says to himself, 'It doesn't look like as though my master will return,' and he begins to mistreat or abuse his fellow servants and to associate with drunks, then the master of that servant will come at a time when he's not expected, and he'll cut him to pieces and assign him a place with the hypocrites where there's deep distress and bitter anger.[161]

Learning of the seeming impossibility of entry into the kingdom of God when Jesus talked of the camel getting through the eye of a needle being easier than a rich man entering the kingdom of God, his disciples, who were astonished at this teaching, asked, "Who then can be saved?"

Looking at them Jesus said, "With man this is impossible, but with God all things are possible."

"We've left everything to follow you," Peter said, "what will be there for us?"

"I'm telling you the truth," Jesus replied, "at the renewal of all things, when the Son of Man sits on his glorious throne, you who have followed me will also sit on twelve thrones judging the twelve tribes of Israel.[162] And everyone who has left houses or family for my sake will receive a hundred times as much and will inherit eternal life. But many who are first will be last, and many who are last will be first."[163] It is God who looks on the heart and knows who belongs to him, and who belong to the enemy.

After that last supper was finished a dispute developed among the disciples as to which of them was considered to be the greatest. Ambition and self-interest was on their mind, and so Jesus said to

---

[161]   Matt 24: 36-51

[162]   Reuben, Simeon, Judah, Issachar, Ephraim, Benjamin, Zebulun, Manasseh, Dan, Asher, Naphtali, Gad.

[163]   Matt 19:24-30

them all, "The kings of the Gentiles use their authority and power over people to make them think that they are great leaders and a benefit to the world, but you're not to be like them, instead, the most senior of you should take the role of the youngest and the one who rules – do it as a servant.

"Is it the person who sits at the table who is the greatest or the one who serves? Is it not the one who sits at the table? Yet I'm with you as a servant. You're the ones who have stood with me in my trials, and I confer on you a kingdom, just as my Father conferred one on me, so that you can eat and drink at my table in my kingdom and sit on thrones, judging the twelve tribes of Israel."[164]

This question of which disciple will receive the top position had come up before, but at that time it had been an ambitious parent that was making the request. It was the mother of James and John who had the nerve to ask Jesus if her sons could sit either side of him in his kingdom.

"You don't know what you're asking," Jesus said to them, as James and John were standing right next to their mother when she made her petition.

Looking at the brothers he asked them, "Can you drink the cup I'm going to drink?"

"We can," they boldly stated.

"You will indeed drink from my cup, but to sit at my side isn't for me to grant. Those positions belong to those whom my Father has chosen."

---

[164]   Luke 22:24-30

The other ten disciples were very angry with James and John, possibly because they were ambitious for those same top positions but hadn't asked.

Jesus talked of the attitude that those who follow him should have; "If anyone wants to follow me they must be prepared to say no to themselves and be ready each day to die for me, because if your primary aim is to save your life you'll lose it, but whoever loses his life for me will save it. What good does it do to gain the whole world and yet lose your life? If anyone is ashamed of me and what I say, the Son of Man will be ashamed of that person when he comes in the glory of the Father and of the holy angels."[165]

There was much religious activity then, as there is now, but Jesus said that Christians are to be careful not to show off their religious devotion. "Be careful not to do your 'acts of righteousness' so that they can be seen; if you do you'll have no reward from your father – so when you give to the needy don't announce it with trumpets, as the hypocrites do in the synagogues and on the streets, to be honoured by men. I'm telling you the truth, they've received their reward in full. But when you give to the needy don't let your left hand know what your right hand is doing, so that your giving is in secret, then your father, who sees what is done in secret, will reward you."[166]

"He who receives you receives me, and he who receives me receives the one who sent me." He went on to say, "Love your enemies, do good to them, and lend to them without expecting to get anything back. Then your reward will be great and you'll be sons of the Most High, because he is kind to the ungrateful and wicked. Be merciful just as your Father is merciful."[167]

---

[165]   Luke 9:23-26

[166]   Matt 6:1-4

[167]   Luke 6:35-36

When Jesus spoke to his disciples of his return he compared it to a man going on a journey that called his servants and entrusted his property to them. To one he gave five talents[168] of money, to another two talents, and to another one talent, each amount suited to the individual. Then the man began his journey.

The one who had received five talents immediately put his money to work and made five more. The one with two talents did the same and made two more talents, but the man with the one talent went away and dug a hole and buried his master's money.

After a long time the master returned and interviewed each of those he gave the money to. The man who made an extra five talents said, "Master, you entrusted me with five talents and look, I've made five more."

"Well done, good and faithful servant," the master replied, "you've been faithful with a few things so come and share your master's happiness!"

The man with the two talents told the master that he too had doubled his money and the master said to him, "Well done, good and faithful servant, as you've been faithful with a few things I'll put you in charge of many things. Come and share your master's happiness."

The man who had been given one talent came and said to the master, "Master, I knew that you're a hard man, harvesting where you've not sown and gathering where you've not scattered seed, so I was afraid and hid your talent in the ground, see, here's what belongs to you."

"You wicked and lazy servant," his master said to him, "so you knew that I harvest where I've not sown and gather where I've not scattered seed? Well, you should've put my money on deposit with

---

[168]   A talent was worth several hundred pounds.

the bank, at least then I could have had it back with interest. Take his talent and give it to the one who has ten talents, because everyone who works with what I've given them will be given more, and then he'll have more than enough. But the person who does nothing with what I give them, even what I've given them will be taken away from them.

"Throw that worthless servant outside into the darkness where there will be great distress and bitter anger."[169]

Seven angels are pictured in the book of Revelation blowing a trumpet, one after the other, and when the seventh angel sounded his trumpet there were loud voices in heaven which said:

"The kingdom of the world has become the kingdom of our Lord and of his Christ, and he will reign forever."

And the twenty-four elders, who were seated on their thrones before God, fell on their faces and worshipped God, saying:

"We give thanks to you, Lord God Almighty, the One who is and who was, because you've taken your great power and have begun to reign. The nations were angry, and your wrath has come. The time has come for judging the dead and for rewarding your servants the prophets and your saints and those who reverence your name, both small and great – and for destroying those who destroy the earth."[170] The time for rewarding the servants of God is still ahead of us.

'Remember those earlier days,' the writer of Hebrews encourages his readers, 'after you had received the light, when you stood your ground in a great contest in the face of suffering. Sometimes you were publicly exposed to insult and persecution; at other times you stood side by side with those who were treated in that way.

---

[169]   Matt 25:14-30

[170]   Rev 11:15-18

You sympathised with those in prison and joyfully accepted the confiscation of your property because you knew that you yourselves had better and lasting possessions.

'So don't throw away your confidence as it will be richly rewarded. You need to persevere so that when you've done the will of God you will receive what he has promised, for in just a very short time "He who is coming will come and will not delay. But the righteous will live by faith, and if he shrinks back I will not be pleased with him."[171] But we're not of those who shrink back and are destroyed but of those who believe and are saved.' A little later he writes, 'without faith it's impossible to please God because anyone who comes to him must believe that he exists and that he rewards those who earnestly seek him.'[172] At the end of this section on the people of faith, we read, 'These were all commended for their faith, yet none of them received what had been promised. God had planned something better for us so that only together with us would they be made perfect.'

All the saints that have died, under the old covenant and under the new covenant, wait in sleep for the time of the King's return so that all together they can receive their reward from him personally. Many wrongly teach that the saved are in heaven enjoying their reward now but this is not consistent with what is written in Scripture. Asaph wrote in one of his psalms, 'You guide me with your council, and afterwards you will take me into glory.' That entering into glory comes at the resurrection. Remember the words of Jesus, "No-one has ever gone in to heaven except the one who came from heaven."[173] Heaven is where God's kingdom comes from, and it will come to earth, but we don't go there to enter it.

---

[171]   Hab 2:3-4

[172]   Heb 10:32-39, 11:6,39-40

[173]   John 3:13

The Messiah and his Father

The first day of the week, Sunday, according to the Hebrew way of counting days, had begun the previous evening. It was still dark and it would be a little while before the sun rose. The small group of women, having observed faithfully the weekly Sabbath were now anxiously nearing the tomb of Jesus.

After the first annual Sabbath ended at sunset on Thursday, they were not able to buy the spices for the body of Jesus that they needed until the following day, which would be Friday, and then they rested on the weekly Sabbath and very early on the first day of the week they made their way in the dark towards the tomb of Jesus knowing that what they intended to do would take some time. Having seen his body being entombed, they wondered between themselves how they were going to be able to move the heavy stone that blocked the entrance to the tomb.

When they got there they saw that the stone had been moved. Entering into the darkness of the tomb they stiffened with shock as they saw what looked like two young men standing on the right side, their clothes radiating a bright light. Alarmed by their presence the women bowed down with their faces to the ground and thought about how they could leave this frightening place when one of these strangers said, "Why do you look for the living among the dead? Don't be scared – you're looking for Jesus, the Nazarene who was crucified and as you can see, he's not here – he's risen from the dead.

Go and tell the disciples and Peter. He's going ahead of you into Galilee, where you'll see him just as he told you."

Nervous and perplexed the women got out of there quickly and because they were afraid they told no-one until later.

Except for one of the women, Mary Magdalene, who hurriedly went to Peter and John and having found them she breathlessly told them that the body of Jesus had gone and they didn't know where it was.

Peter and John went running to the tomb, and John got there first. He lowered himself to look inside but didn't go in, while Peter having arrived moved past John and went inside. They both saw the strips of linen that had been around the body and the burial cloth that had covered his head. They said nothing but thought it strange that if somebody had taken the body why were the burial cloth and linen still there? What was even stranger was that the linen sheets and the cloth were rolled up and neatly placed on the side of where the body had lain.

Peter and John then went back to where they were staying still not grasping what had happened. Mary remained at the entrance to the tomb crying. She bent over to look once more into the tomb and saw the same two men dressed in white now sitting where Jesus' body had been and they asked her, "Woman, why are you crying?"

"They've taken my Lord away, and I don't know where they've put him," she said. In her frustration she turned and saw a man who she supposed was the gardener and he asked her the same question, "Woman, why are you crying? Who are you looking for?"

"Sir," she pleaded, "if you've carried him away – tell me where you've put him and I'll get him."

"Mary." He said.

She looked at him through tear filled eyes and recognised his familiar voice. She cried out, "Rabboni!"[174] She rushed towards him and held him tightly. She had lost him once, but never again would anyone take him from her. Looking directly at her he reassuringly said, "There's no need to keep hold of me because I still have to return to the Father but you go and tell my brothers, 'I am returning to my Father and your Father, to my God and your God.'"

Mary went to the disciples and full of joy told them; "I have seen the Lord!" She then told them what had happened and what Jesus had told her.

Jesus called God his God and his Father. Attempting to understand that simple statement was later to cause deep division and bitter arguments between the bishops of the West and the bishops of the East during the next few centuries, and differences over one letter of one word would be sufficient for bishops on either side of this disagreement to be excommunicated.

The Greek word was *Homoousios*, but there was also the word *Homoiousios*. Some supported the first word and some supported the second word, but there were others who rejected both words. These words were employed to describe the relationship between the Father and the Son. This contentious issue came down to the question; is the Son 'like' the Father, or the 'same' as the Father? As interesting as this topic may be, the problem was that once one of these words was accepted as the orthodox teaching of the church those holding a different theological position were then classified as heretics, and would face the law of the state which worked hand in glove with the church.

Ivor J. Davidson, writing in his second volume of church history[175] says, '*Homoousios* was, however, a word with a difficult

---

[174]   An Aramaic term showing a greater respect than just 'Rabbi'

[175]   'A Public Faith' The Monarch history of the church, page 35.

history. For a start, it was not biblical, which meant that the council (of Nicaea, AD 325) was proposing to talk about the nature of the Godhead in terms that were philosophical or conceptual rather than in language drawn directly from the Scriptures.'

David F. Wright, speaking of the period when the early creeds were formulated writes,[176] 'At the same time it was an age of interference and even domination by the emperors, of colourful and abrasive personalities, and bitter antagonism between leading bishoprics. Technical terms without biblical origins were made key-words in authoritative statements of belief. Their use contributed to the Latin-speaking West and the Greek-speaking East misunderstanding and misrepresenting one another. Even between different segments of the Greek church misunderstandings arose; these disputes contributed to major division in the Christian world.

'In theory the first appeal was to Scripture, but the Bible was used in curious or questionable ways. People frequently appealed to Scripture to confirm their theology rather than to decide it. Above all, the disputes were shot through with the feeling that unless God and Christ were truly what Christian devotion and worship claimed, then salvation itself was endangered. Passions ran high because the fundamentals of the Christian religion were felt to be at stake.'

The councils of the early church went into areas that the Bible doesn't specifically address because the reality of the spiritual life that God and Jesus share is beyond human comprehension and all words or combinations of words will fall short of touching that reality. The Bible is concerned, not with explaining how that holy and spiritual dimension works, but in the love and unity between God the Father and Jesus the Son.

---

[176]   ' The History of Christianity' A Lion Handbook, Councils and Creeds, page 164.

The various creeds which are considered so fundamental and of such importance in this world came not from God but from the minds of those who were greatly influenced by the philosophical writings that preceded them. And because their decisions were used as a type of litmus test of who is a real Christian and who is not, they have divided people rather than bringing them together; instead of breaking down a dividing wall of hostility they have erected and strengthened one wall after another, which, as all can see, presents to the world a divided and factious Christianity that is a counterfeit of the reality of Christian unity.

In the face of so many creeds, statements of beliefs and confessions of faith what was needed was there all along; the words of Jesus himself. As Peter said to Jesus, "Lord, to whom shall we go? You have the words of eternal life and we believe and know that you are the Holy One of God."[177]

It's natural to want to understand all the spiritual truths in depth and to get answers to all our questions concerning spiritual matters so we should appreciate every lack of understanding, as well as the misunderstandings, that the disciples expressed because that gave Jesus the opportunity to explain to them, and to us, what we wouldn't otherwise know.

"All things have been committed to me by my Father. No-one knows the Son except the father, and no-one knows the Father except the Son and those to whom the Son chooses to reveal him."[178]

Many Christians are encouraged to study and memorise one of the creeds so as to know the central beliefs and to defend the truth from error, but Jesus says, "Come to me, all you who are weary and burdened, and I'll give you rest. Take my yoke and make it yours and

---

[177]   John 6:68-69

[178]   Matt 11:27

learn from me, because I'm gentle and my heart is humble, and you'll find rest for your lives. My yoke is easy and my burden is light."

The easy and best way is to listen to him and put into practice what he says; the hard way is to listen to what many of this world's church authorities teach and be duped with it. John writes, 'God did not send his Son into the world to condemn the world, but to save the world through him. Whoever believes in him is not condemned, but whoever does not believe stands condemned already because he has not believed in the name of God's one and only Son.'[179]

Jesus spoke to his disciples about his Father; "The Father himself loves you because you've loved me and have believed that I came from God. I came from the Father and entered the world; now I'm leaving the world and going back to the Father."[180]

In Luke's genealogy of Jesus going all the way back to the first man, Adam is called 'the son of God.' All those who come to believe Jesus as the Son of God, themselves become God's children,[181] as when writing of the creation Job says, 'when the morning stars sang together and all the sons of God (angels) shouted for joy.'[182]

Moses was instructed by God to tell Pharaoh that "Israel is my firstborn son."[183] Hosea, writing seven centuries before the birth of Jesus, wrote, 'When Israel was a child, I loved him, and out of Egypt I called my son.'[184] After the death of King Herod the parents of Jesus, who had taken him to Egypt for safety, were told that they could

---

[179]   John 3:17-18

[180]   John 16:27-28

[181]   John 1:12-13

[182]   Job 38:7

[183]   Ex 4:22

[184]   Hos 11:1

return to Israel and so Matthew in his account sees that saying of Hosea as being fulfilled in Jesus' stay in Egypt.

David, the king, was told by God, through the prophet Nathan, that his son, who would succeed him, would build a house for God, and that God would be his Father and he would be God's son. In the second Psalm David writes, 'He said to me, "You are my Son; today I have become your Father. Ask me, and I will make the nations your inheritance, the ends of the earth. You will rule over them with an iron sceptre; you will dash them to pieces like pottery." The writer of Hebrews picks up the these two quotes[185] and applies them to Jesus, and goes on to write, 'But we see Jesus, who was made a little lower than the angels, now crowned with glory and honour because he suffered death, so that by the grace of God he might taste death for everyone.'

John the Baptist said of Jesus, "The one whom God sent speaks the words of God, for God gives the Spirit without limit. The Father loves the Son and has placed everything in his hands. Whoever believes in the Son has eternal life, but whoever rejects the Son will not see life because God's wrath remains on him."[186]

Jesus told those who were his enemies, "You are of this world but I'm not of this world. I told you that you would die in your sins – if you don't believe that I am the one I claim to be – you will indeed die in your sins. I'm telling you the truth, whoever listens to what I say and believes him who sent me has eternal life and will not be condemned." In answer to their question, 'Who are you?' he said, "I am what I've been claiming all along. I've much to say in judgment of you, but he who sent me is reliable, and what I've heard from him I tell the world."

---

[185]   Also Psa 45:6-7, 110:1, 102:25-27.

[186]   John 3:34-36

They didn't understand that he was telling them about his Father, so Jesus said, "When you've lifted up the Son of Man, then you'll know that I am the one I claim to be and that I do nothing on my own but speak what the Father has taught me. The one who sent me is with me; he has not left me alone because I always do what pleases him." While he was speaking many put their trust in him.

The Jews called him a Samaritan[187]and demon-possessed; he had just said to them that their father wasn't God but that Satan was, because they belonged to him.

"I'm not possessed by a demon," Jesus replied, "but I honour my Father and you dishonour me. I'm not looking for glory for myself, but there is one who is concerned with it and he is the judge. I'm telling you the truth, if anyone keeps my word, he will never see death."

"Now we definitely know that you're demon-possessed!" the people replied, "Abraham is dead as well as all the prophets and yet you say that if anyone keeps your word, he will never taste death." Their anger was rising. "Are you greater than our father Abraham? He died and so did the prophets, so who do you think you are?"

"If I glorify myself, my glory means nothing. My Father, who you claim as your God, is the one who glorifies me, though you don't know him, but I do. If I said I didn't I would be a liar like you, but I do know him and keep his word. Your father Abraham rejoiced at the thought of seeing my day and he was glad when he saw it."

This was too much for those he was addressing. "You're not yet fifty years old and you've seen Abraham!"

"I'm telling you the truth, before Abraham was born, I am!" There was a moment's silence as the enormity of what he had said sunk in,

---

[187]   This was because Jesus had gone against the traditions of the elders.

then, incensed by what they had heard they picked up the stones that were there, as building work on the temple was still going on, and they fully intended to stone him there and then but God protected him because his time to die was not to be that day.

When Moses was confronted by an angel speaking on behalf of God in flames of fire from within a bush he asked, "Suppose I go to the Israelites and say to them, 'The God of your fathers has sent me to you,' and they ask me, 'What is his name?' Then what shall I tell them?"

God said to Moses, "I AM WHO I AM. This is what you're to say to the Israelites; I AM has sent me to you.' Say to them, 'The Lord,[188] the God of your fathers – the God of Abraham, the God of Isaac and the God of Jacob – has sent me to you.' This is my name forever, the name by which I am to be remembered from generation to generation."

This is why the Jews wanted to kill Jesus. In their eyes he was worthy of death because he had taken the name of God and applied it to himself when he said, 'before Abraham was born I am!' This, for them, was blatant blasphemy.

Paul, writing to the Corinthians, said, 'I don't want you to be ignorant of the fact, brothers, that our forefathers were all under the cloud and that they all passed through the sea. They were all baptised into Moses in the cloud and in the sea. They all ate the same spiritual food and drank the same spiritual drink; because they drank from the spiritual rock that accompanied them, and that rock was Christ. Nevertheless, God was not pleased with most of them and their bodies were scattered over the desert.'

---

[188]   God was formally known as *El Shaddai,* meaning 'God Almighty. The 'Lord,' *Yahweh,* sounds like and may be derived from the Hebrew for *I AM.*

The Lord who spoke to Moses and provided for the people of Israel was the one who 1200 years later was born in Bethlehem. He was protected and led by his Father of whom he said, "I and the Father are one."

On that last night with his disciples Philip asked Jesus, "Lord, show us the Father and that will be enough for us."

"Don't you know me Philip, even after I've been among you such a long time? Anyone who has seen me has seen the Father so how can you say, 'Show us the Father'? Don't you believe that I'm in the Father and that the Father is in me? The words that I say to you are not just my own; it's the Father living in me who is doing the work.

Believe me when I say that I am in the Father and the Father is in me or at least believe on the evidence of the miracles themselves."

He went on to say, "I am the true vine and my Father is the gardener. He cuts off every branch that doesn't bear fruit while every branch that does bear fruit he prunes and cleans so that it will be even more fruitful. You are already clean because of what I have told you. Remain in me and I will remain in you. No branch can bear fruit by itself; it must remain in the vine. Neither can you bear fruit unless you remain in me.

"If you don't remain in me you'll be like a branch that's thrown away and withers; such branches are picked up, thrown into the fire and burned. If you obey my commands you will remain in my love just as I have obeyed my Father's commands and remain in his love. I've told you this so that my joy may be in you and that your joy may be complete. My command is that you love each other as I have loved you."[189]

---

[189]   John 15:1-4, 9-12

Paul wrote in his letter to Timothy, 'I charge you to keep this command without spot or blame until the appearing of our Lord Jesus Christ, which God will bring about in his own time – God, the blessed and only Ruler, King of kings and Lord of lords, who alone is immortal and who lives in unapproachable light, whom no-one has seen or can see. To him be honour and might forever. Amen.'[190]

In the book of Revelation the same expression 'King of kings and Lord of lords' is used twice, and they both refer to Jesus. Speaking in highly symbolic language of a military force that will oppose Jesus at his return, we read, 'They will make war against the lamb, but the lamb will overcome them because he is Lord of lords and King of kings – and with him will be his called, chosen and faithful followers.'[191] And a little later John writes, 'I saw heaven standing open and there before me was a white horse, whose rider is called Faithful and True. With justice he judges and makes war. His eyes are like blazing fire and on his head are many crowns. He has a name written on him that no-one knows but he himself. He is dressed in a robe dipped in blood and his name is the Word of God. The armies of heaven were following him, riding on white horses and dressed in fine linen, white and clean. Out of his mouth comes a sharp sword with which to strike down the nations. He will rule them with an iron sceptre. He treads the winepress of the fury of the wrath of God Almighty. On his robe and on his thigh he has this name written: KING OF KINGS AND LORD OF LORDS.[192]

This blending of the titles of God the Father and Jesus the Son is evidence of a unique love and unity that is shared between them. The many promises of the coming Messiah found in the Old Testament also display the same unity of titles. Isaiah wrote; 'For to us a child is born, to us a son is given, and the government will be on his

---

[190]   1 Tim 6:13b-16

[191]   Rev 17:14

[192]   Rev 19:11-16

shoulders, and he will be called Wonderful Counsellor, Mighty God, Everlasting Father, Prince of Peace. Of the increase of his government and peace there will be no end. He will reign on David's throne and over his kingdom, establishing and upholding it with justice and righteousness from that time on forever.'[193]

Paul, writing about the resurrection to the Corinthians, makes it clear that the Messiah is subject to God. Paul is teaching how there is a sequence beginning with the Messiah's resurrection and then, at his return, 'those who belong to him, then the end will come, when he hands over the kingdom to God the Father after he has destroyed all dominion, authority and power because he must reign until he has put all his enemies under his feet. The last enemy to be destroyed is death.

'For he has put everything under his feet.[194]Now when it says that "everything" has been put under him, it's clear that this doesn't include God himself, who put everything under the Messiah. When he has done this, then the Son himself will be made subject to him who put everything under him so that God may be all in all.'[195]

Earlier in the same letter Paul had written, 'for us there is but one God, the Father, from whom all things came and for whom we live; and there is but one Lord, Jesus Christ, through whom all things came and through whom we live.'[196]

Paul further calls God 'our Saviour, who wants all men to be saved and to come to a knowledge of the truth. For there is one God and

---

[193]   Isa 9:6-7

[194]   Psa 8:6

[195]   1 Cor 15:23-28

[196]   1 Cor 8:6

one mediator between God and men, the man Christ Jesus, who gave himself as a ransom for all men.'[197]

At the beginning of each of Paul's letters he uses a similar framework in addressing his readers. To each church location he includes the phrase 'in God the Father and the Lord Jesus Christ,' or a benediction 'from God the Father and Christ Jesus our Lord.' While there is a greater unity between the Father and the Son than any human can experience there is also a difference that in our present human state we cannot fully comprehend. This is why what the early church authorities demanded in making a set formula of words mandatory on all Christians was going beyond what Scripture teaches us, and directly led to the suffering of many thousands of people, and also set in stone the things of which Paul said that we don't at this time see clearly. This forcing of people to accept as law what the church taught was not from God but from the prince of this world.

Paul advised Timothy to warn God's people against quarrelling about words. 'It's of no value, and only ruins those who listen.'[198] Yet that is exactly what the early church leaders got their theological teeth into, and engaged in a good deal of biting each other in the process.[199] This conflict and division was set to continue down through the centuries and is still with us.

At that last Passover meal with his disciples, Jesus prayed for them as they very soon were to experience a deeply traumatic period of time and then his mind turned to all those who would come to have faith in him through the following decades and centuries:

---

[197]   1 Tim 2:3-6

[198]   2 Tim 2:14

[199]   Gal 5:15

"My prayer isn't for them alone. I also pray for those who will believe in me through their message, that all of them may be one. Father, just as you are in me and I am in you, may they also be in us so that the world may believe that you've sent me. I have given them the glory that you gave me, that they may be one as we are: I in them and you in me. May they be brought to complete unity to let the world know that you sent me and have loved them as you have loved me.

"Father, I want those you've given me to be with me where I am, and to see my glory, the glory you've given me because you loved me before the creation of the world. Righteous Father, though the world doesn't know you, I know you, and they know that you've sent me. I've made you known to them, and will continue to make you known in order that the love you have for me may be in them and that I myself may be in them."[200]

---

[200]   John 17:20-26

The Messiah and blindness

Jesus and his disciples came across a man who had been blind from birth,[201]and he was asked, "Teacher, who caused this blindness? Was it this man who sinned or was it his parents who sinned?"

This belief that if a person is suffering then sin isn't far off was the charge Job's friends laid at his feet. He felt that not only his friends were against him but God himself was after him. Job gave full vent to what he saw as an injustice; "I loathe my life and so I'll give free rein to my complaint and speak out in my bitterness.[202]

"I'll say to God: Don't condemn me, but tell me what charges you have against me. Does it please you to oppress me – to spurn the work of your hands, while you smile on the schemes of the wicked?

"Do you have eyes of flesh? Do you see as a mortal sees?

"Are your days like those of a mortal or your years like those of a man, that you must search out my faults and probe after my sin – though you know that I am not guilty and that no-one can rescue me from your hand?

"Your hands shaped me and made me. Will you now turn and destroy me? Remember that you moulded me like clay. Will you now

---

[201]   John 9

[202]   Job 10

turn me to dust again? Did you not pour me out like milk and curdle me like cheese, clothe me with skin and flesh and knit me together with bones and sinews?

"You gave me life and showed me kindness, and in your providence watched over my spirit. But this is what you concealed in your heart, and I know that this was in your mind. If I sinned, you would be watching me and would not let my offence go unpunished. If I am guilty – woe to me! Even if I am innocent, I cannot lift my head, for I am full of shame and drowned in my affliction.

"If I hold my head high, you stalk me like a lion and again display your awesome power against me. You bring new witnesses against me and increase your anger towards me; your forces come against me, wave upon wave.

"Why then did you bring me out of the womb? I wish I had died before any eye saw me. If only I had never come into being, or had been carried straight from the womb to the grave!

"Are not my few days almost over? Turn away from me so that I can have a moment's joy before I go to the place of no return, to the land of gloom and deep shadow, to the land of deepest night, of deep shadow and disorder, where even the light is like darkness."

While Job tortured himself with these thoughts his close friends attempted to reason with him by telling him that he is only getting what he deserved and that if he were innocent his life would be full of blessings and one of them underlined this by saying; "Is not your wickedness great? Are not your sins endless?" The great difficulty Job had in accepting this charge was that it wasn't true. The first lines of the book of Job have; 'In the Land of Uz[203]there lived a man whose name was Job. This man was blameless and upright; he feared

---

[203]   Nobody knows where this is. It is possible that Moses wrote this challenging book.

God and shunned evil.' So understanding why people suffer goes far beyond any particular sin having been committed.

The disciples, on seeing this man who had been blind from birth, assumed that sin, directly the man's, or indirectly, his parents, was responsible for this man's state.

To their surprise Jesus told them that neither this man nor his parents sinned.[204] "This happened," Jesus said, "so that the work of God might be displayed in his life. As long as it's day, we must do the work of him who sent me. Night is coming when no-one can work. While I'm in the world I'm the light of the world."

Jesus then spat on the ground and made some paste with his saliva, and he put it on the man's eyes. "Go and wash in the Pool of Siloam" (this word means Sent). The man went to the pool and after washing his eyes, went home seeing.

Those who knew him, including his own neighbours, and had seen him begging, were sure that he and this sighted man were one and the same man, but others considered he wasn't that man; he just looked like him.

"I am the man," he insisted.

"How were your eyes opened?" they demanded.

"The man called Jesus made some paste and put it on my eyes and he told me to go to Siloam and wash, so that's what I did and then I could see!"

"Where is this man?"

"I don't know," he answered.

---

[204]   'Sinned' in regard to the man's blindness because all have sinned; 'all have sinned,' Rom 3:23.

The Pharisees were the authority on the law and its interpretation and so the man who was blind was taken to them. The healing had taken place on the Sabbath. Now it was their turn to ask the questions. He answered them in the same way he answered his friends and neighbours.

"This man isn't from God," some of the Pharisees concluded, "because he doesn't keep the Sabbath."

"How can a sinner do such miraculous signs?" others countered. Neither side could agree so they turned again to the man who had been blind.

"What have you got to say about him? It was your eyes he opened."

"He's a prophet," the man replied.

The Jews still didn't believe that he had been blind and decided to interview his parents to establish the truth. When his parents arrived they asked them if he were their son. When they said he was, the Pharisees went on to ask some further questions.

"Is this the one you say was born blind? How is it that he can now see?"

"Of course he is our son, but how he can now see, or who opened his eyes, we don't know. Ask him, he's an adult – he can speak for himself."

They said this because they were afraid of the Pharisees because they had already agreed that anyone who acknowledged that Jesus was the Messiah would be put out of the synagogue.

For a second time they summoned the man who had been blind and strongly urged him to give God the glory because they knew that this pretender is a sinner.

"Whether he's a sinner or not, I don't know, but one thing I do know, I was blind but now I see!"

"What did he do to you? How did he open your eyes?"

"I've told you already and you didn't listen. Why do you want to hear it again? Do you want to become his disciples too?"

"You're this stranger's disciple! We're disciples of Moses! We know that God spoke to Moses, as for this person, we don't even know where he came from."

"Now that's remarkable! You don't know where he comes from yet he opened my eyes. We know that God doesn't listen to sinners – he listens to the godly person who does his will. Nobody has ever heard of opening the eyes of a man born blind. If this man were not from God he could do nothing."

"You were steeped in sin at birth," they reacted with insults. "How dare you lecture us!" At that they threw him out.

When Jesus heard that he had been thrown out he went to find him and when he was found Jesus said to him, "Do you believe in the Son of Man?"

"Who is he, sir? Tell me so that I may believe in him."

"You've seen him; in fact, he's speaking to you now."

"Lord," the man responded, "I believe," and he worshipped him.

Jesus then spoke to those around him, "For judgment I've come into this world, so that the blind will see and those who see will become blind."

There were some Pharisees with him who didn't like what they heard and so they asked Jesus, "What? Are we blind too?"

"If you were blind," Jesus said to them, "you wouldn't be guilty of sin; but because you claim you can see, your guilt remains."

Paul, a former Pharisee, in writing to the Romans, spoke of that legalistic frame of mind which saw the fulfilling of the requirements of the law as the way to achieve righteousness before God. He wrote, 'Now you, if you call yourself a Jew and brag about your relationship with God; if you know his will and approve of what is superior because you are instructed by the law; if you are convinced that you are a guide for the blind, a light for those who are in the dark, an instructor of the foolish, a teacher of infants because you have in the law the embodiment of knowledge and truth – you, then, who teach others, do you not teach yourself?'[205]

They considered themselves as 'guides for the blind', but Jesus called them, "blind guides",[206] and posed the question, "can a blind man lead a blind man? Will they not both fall into a pit?" God cares for the blind. Moses wrote, 'Cursed is the man who leads the blind astray on the road.'[207] And the Psalmist wrote, 'The Lord sets prisoners free, the Lord gives sight to the blind.'[208]

Isaiah wrote of a time when, 'In that day the deaf will hear the words of the scroll, and out of gloom and darkness the eyes of the blind will see.'[209]

---

[205] Rom 2:17-21. They were teaching that a man must be circumcised to be acceptable before God.

[206] Matt 23:16, Luke 6:39

[207] Deut 27:18

[208] Psa 146:7b-8a

[209] Isa 29:18

One Sabbath, when Jesus was in the synagogue at Nazareth, he was given the scroll of Isaiah to read from, and unrolling it he came to the place where it is written: "The Spirit of the Lord is on me because he has anointed me to preach good news to the poor. He has sent me to proclaim freedom for the prisoners and recovery of sight for the blind, to release the oppressed, to proclaim the year of the Lord's favour."[210]

This is freedom from spiritual oppression and spiritual blindness. When he healed people of what was afflicting them it was small tokens of what in the future the whole world would experience – not by a church or a charismatic leader in highly dubious healings, but when he returns to liberate the blind and the oppressed – all of us. Jesus quoted, in part, from where Isaiah speaks of what God's servant will do: "I, the Lord, have called you in righteousness; I will take hold of your hand. I will keep you and will make you to be a covenant for the people and a light for the Gentiles, to open eyes that are blind, to free captives from prison and to release from the dungeon those who sit in darkness." He goes on to say, "I will lead the blind by ways they have not known, along unfamiliar paths I will guide them; I will turn the darkness into light before them and make the rough places smooth.[211]

John wrote that 'anyone who claims to be in the light but hates his brother is still in the darkness. Whoever loves his brother lives in the light, and there's nothing in it to make him stumble, but whoever hates his brother is in the darkness and walks around in the darkness; he doesn't know where he's going, because the darkness has blinded him.' John had earlier written, 'This is the message we've heard from him and declare to you: God is light; in him there is no darkness at all.'[212]

---

[210]   Luke 4:18-19

[211]   Isa 42:6-7, 16.

[212]   1John 2:9-11, 1:5.

In the letter addressed to the Laodiceans, found in the book of Revelation, Jesus gives them the reality of their spiritual condition. "These are the words of the Amen, the faithful and true witness, the ruler of God's creation. I know your deeds, that you are neither hot nor cold. I wish you were either one or the other! So, because you're lukewarm – neither hot nor cold – I am about to spit you out of my mouth.

"You say, 'I'm rich; I've acquired wealth and don't need a thing.' But you don't realise that you're wretched, pitiful, poor, blind and naked. I counsel you to buy from me gold refined in the fire, so that you can become rich; and white clothes to wear, so that you can cover your shameful nakedness; and salve to put on your eyes, so that you can see.

"Those whom I love I rebuke and discipline. So be earnest, and repent. Here I am! I stand at the door and knock. If anyone hears my voice and opens the door, I will come in and eat with him, and he with me.

"To him who overcomes, I will give the right to sit with me on my throne, just as I overcame and sat down with my Father on his throne. He who has an ear, let him hear what the Spirit says to the churches."[213]

The Pharisees were blind in their insistence on regulations and rituals, and blind to the Son of God when he was among them; 'He came to that which was his own, but his own did not receive him.'[214]The churches today can be just as blind as the Pharisees were in insisting on their own distinctive regulations and rituals, and just as blind to the real Messiah as his own people were. Jesus turns his critical gaze over his people and rebukes, corrects and counsels, as he did to the Christians at Laodicea who had become lukewarm which

---

[213]   Rev 3:14-22

[214]   John 1:11

made it imperative that they repent and listen to his voice. He then ends his message to them with an incredible promise of sitting with him on his throne, just as he sits on God's throne.

If we listen, there is both the discipline of a father to a son and the promise of 'a harvest of righteousness and peace for those who have been trained by it.'[215]

Some fellowships are targeted for their deviation from Scripture and their non-biblical texts that are treated as Scripture – these are easy targets but it's far more difficult to see Scriptural error in our own fellowship, because we don't believe we have any. The spiritual blindness that we clearly see in others goes further and deeper than any of us have realised.

---

[215]   Heb 12:11

The Messiah and the human heart

Jeremiah wrote, 'The heart is deceitful above all things and beyond cure. Who can understand it? I the Lord search the heart and examine the mind, to reward a person according to their conduct, according to what their deeds deserve.'[216]

The Psalmist says, 'The Lord looks down from heaven on humans to see if there are any who understand, any who seek God. All have turned aside, they have together become corrupt; there is no-one who does good, not even one.'[217]

One day a young rich man who had a leadership role in his community ran up to Jesus and dropped to his knees in front of him. "Good teacher," he respectfully asked, "what must I do to inherit eternal life?"

"Why do you call me good?" Jesus unexpectedly asked. Then he made an extraordinary statement.

"No-one is good – except God alone..." then Jesus began to show this man that his high opinion of himself could be punctured by being asked to leave his money to others and then, left with nothing, but his faith, to follow Jesus. This he could not do. Many people when asked, 'do you think that you are a good person?' would answer, 'yes,'

---

[216]   Jer 17:9-10

[217]   Psa 14:2-3

not knowing either themselves or what Jesus said about our human condition.

Jesus had been encouraging his disciples to be bold and persistent when they pray, and said, "So I say to you: Ask and it will be given to you; seek and you will find; knock and the door will be opened to you, because everyone who asks receives; he who seeks finds; and to him who knocks, the door will be opened.

"Which of you fathers, if your child asks for a fish, will give him a snake instead? Or if the child asks for an egg, will a scorpion be given? If you then, though you are evil, know how to give good gifts to your children, how much more will your father in heaven give the Holy Spirit to those who ask him!"[218]

When Jesus referred to his disciples as evil he was including them with all of humanity as we all share the same sinful human nature.

Before the flood it is recorded that 'the Lord saw how great man's wickedness on earth had become, and that every inclination of the thoughts of his heart was only evil all the time.' The flood that destroyed all but eight people showed God's hostility to evil but human nature had not changed when those eight left the ark.

Before Israel entered the land that God had promised them, Moses wrote that they were to annihilate those various tribes that lived there because of the evil that they were doing. But, 'after the Lord your God has driven them out before you, do not say to yourself, "The Lord has brought me here to take possession of this land because of my righteousness." No, it's on account of the wickedness of these nations that the Lord is going to drive them out before you. It's not because of your righteousness or your integrity that you are going in to take possession of their land; but on account of the wickedness of these nations, the Lord your God will drive them out before you,

---

[218]   Luke 11:9-13

to accomplish what he swore to your fathers, to Abraham, Isaac and Jacob. Understand, then, that it's not because of your righteousness that the Lord your God is giving you this good land to possess, because you are a rebellious and stubborn people.

'Remember this and never forget how you provoked the Lord your God to anger in the desert. From the day you left Egypt until you arrived here, you have been rebellious against the Lord.'[219]

Out of the approximately three million people who left Egypt only two, who were twenty and over at that time, crossed the River Jordan from the Plains of Moab, east of Jericho, forty years later.

David wrote in the Psalms, 'The Lord is close to the broken-hearted and saves those who are crushed in spirit.'[220]When Jesus spoke of the blessed state of the 'poor in spirit' he was referring to their humility, not the state of their bank balance, because there were many who liked to think that they were close to God, such as the Pharisees who came to Jesus and asked, "Why do your disciples break the tradition of the elders when they don't wash their hands before eating?"

"And why do you break the command of God for the sake of your tradition?" Jesus replied, "God said, 'Honour your father and mother' and 'Anyone who curses his father or mother must be put to death' but you say that if a man says to his father or mother, 'Whatever help you might otherwise have received from me is a gift devoted to God,' he is not to 'honour his father' with it. In so doing you nullify the word of God for the sake of your tradition. You hypocrites! Isaiah was right when he prophesied about you: 'These people honour me with their lips, but their hearts are far from me. They worship me in vain; their teachings are but rules taught by men.'"

---

[219]   Deut 9:4-7

[220]   Psa 34:18

Then Jesus called the crowd to him and said, "Listen and understand. What goes into a man's mouth doesn't make him 'unclean', but what comes out of his mouth, that's what makes him 'unclean.'"

The disciples told him, "The Pharisees were offended by what you said."

"Every plant that my heavenly Father has not planted will be pulled up by the roots. Leave them, because they're blind guides, and if a blind man leads a blind man they'll both fall into a ditch."

"Explain this parable to us," Peter asked.

"Are you still so dull? Don't you see that whatever enters the mouth goes into the stomach and then out of the body? But the things that come out of the mouth come from the heart, and these make a man 'unclean'. Because out of the heart come these evil thoughts, murder, adultery, sexual immorality, theft, false testimony and slander. These are what make a man 'unclean', but eating with unwashed hands doesn't make him 'unclean'."[221]

When a person comes to realise that they are 'unclean' they know that they need cleaning. These terms were used by David in one of his Psalms when the prophet Nathan came to him after David had committed adultery with Bathsheba:

'Have mercy on me, O God, according to your unfailing love; according to your great compassion blot out my transgression. Wash away all my iniquity and cleanse me from my sin...cleanse me with hyssop, and I shall be clean; wash me, and I will be whiter than snow.

'Let me hear joy and gladness; let the bones you have crushed rejoice. Hide your face from my sins and blot out all my iniquity. Create in me a pure heart, O God, and renew a steadfast spirit within

---

[221]   Matt 15:1-20

me. Do not cast from your presence or take your Holy Spirit from me. Restore to me the joy of your salvation and grant me a willing spirit to sustain me.'[222]

Ezekiel writes of a future cleansing for the people of God: "I will sprinkle clean water on you, and you will be clean; I will cleanse you from all your impurities and from all your idols. I will give you a new heart and put a new spirit in you; I will remove from you your heart of stone and give you a heart of flesh.[223]

Isaiah wrote of the change that comes from this divine cleansing; "Come now, let's reason together," says the Lord. "Though your sins are like scarlet, they shall be as white as snow; though they're red as crimson, they'll be like wool. If you're willing and obedient, you'll eat the best from the land; but if you resist and rebel, you'll be devoured by the sword."[224]

When, just before the Passover dinner, Jesus washed the feet of his disciples to give them the example of a master washing the feet of his servants, which would demonstrate the humility that his disciples must show to each other, that washing had a even greater significance beyond that act of humble service.

The evening meal was being served, and the devil had already prompted Judas Iscariot, son of Simon, to betray Jesus. Jesus knew that the Father had put all things under his power, and that he had come from God and was returning to God; so he got up from the meal, took off his outer clothing, and wrapped a towel round his waist. Then he poured water into a basin and began to wash his disciples' feet, drying them with the towel that was wrapped round him.

"Lord," Peter said to him, "are you going to wash my feet?"

---

[222]   Psa 51:1-2, 7-12.

[223]   Ezek 36:25-26

[224]   Isa 1:18-20

"You don't realise now what I'm doing, but later you'll understand," Jesus told him.

"No," Peter protested, "you'll never wash my feet."

"Unless I wash you, you'll have no part with me," Jesus firmly said.

"Lord," Peter responded, "then not just my feet but my hands and head as well!"

"A person who's had a bath needs only to wash his feet as his body is clean, and you are clean, though not every one of you." Jesus knew who was going to betray him – that was why he said not everyone was clean.[225]

When sin entered the world death was its consequence. Sin is ingrained into our human nature which is hostile to God and not submissive to his law. The sinful nature is set on what that nature wants and is the way of death. Death came through Adam and all who came from him die. Adam was commanded not to eat from the tree of the knowledge of good and evil, because if he did he would incur the death sentence.

When he decided to eat that fruit he did it knowingly and willingly, and when God challenged him to explain why he disobeyed the command not to, Adam shifted the blame to the woman, whom God had given him, so, in Adam's reasoning, God was to blame for what had happened. But God held the man responsible and said to him, "Because you listened to your wife and ate from the tree about which I commanded you, 'You must not eat it,' cursed is the ground because of you; through painful work you will eat from it all the days of your life.

---

[225]   John 13:2-11

"It will produce thorns and thistles for you and you will eat the plants of the field. By the sweat of your brow you will eat your food until you return to the ground, since you were taken from it, because you are of the earth and to the earth you will return."[226]

Paul, in writing to the Christians at Romans, says, 'in this way death came to all men, because all sinned. Before the Law was given to Moses sin was in the world even though it hadn't been written down. Even so, death reigned from the time of Adam to the time of Moses even though they didn't break any specific command as Adam did. Adam was a type of the one to come (the first man became a living being, the last Adam, a life-giving spirit. The spiritual didn't come first, but the natural, and after that the spiritual. The first man was of the earth, the second man from heaven[227]).

The contrast between the first and last Adam is absolute. It is the contrast between life and death, obedience and disobedience, condemnation and justification. The gift of God is eternal life and the wages of sin is death, but the gift isn't like the consequences of the sin because just as many died by that one sin of Adam many more are recipients of that gift which came by God's grace through the one man Jesus the Messiah.

The gift of God stands in contrast to the result of the one man's sin. The judgment that followed that one act of disobedience brought condemnation, but the gift followed many sins and brought justification. Because of one man's sin death reigned through that one man, but for those who receive God's abundant provision of grace and the gift of righteousness they will reign in life through the one man, Jesus the Messiah.

As the result of Adam's sin all were condemned to die, but, as a result of one act of righteousness, justification came which brings life

---

[226]   Gen 2:17, 3:11-12, 17-19

[227]   1 Cor 15:45-47

to all. Many became sinners because of Adam's sin but because of the obedience of the one man many will be made righteous.[228]

Paul goes on to write, 'count yourselves dead to sin but alive to God in the Messiah Jesus. So don't let sin reign in your mortal body so that you obey its evil desires, and don't offer yourselves as an instruments for sin, but offer yourselves to God as those who have been brought from death to life and give yourselves to him as instruments of righteousness, because sin shall not be your master – you're no longer under the sentence of the law, but under the grace that has freed you.'

Paul taught that we should be circumcised, not physically, but inwardly; of the heart, not by a written code but by God's Spirit.[229] Moses said the same thing, "Circumcise your hearts and don't be stiff-necked any longer."[230]

Jesus said, "No good tree bears bad fruit, nor does a bad tree bear good fruit. Each tree is recognised by its own fruit. People don't pick figs from thorn-bushes or grapes from briers. The good man brings good things out of the good stored up in his heart, and the evil man brings evil out of the evil stored up in his heart, because out of the overflow of his heart he speaks."[231]

Jesus knew human nature and so neither entrusted himself to men or needed to learn anything from them. He knew what we are on the inside.

Our human nature is impossible to change, but God does the impossible.

---

[228]   Rom 5:12-19, my paraphrase.

[229]   Rom 2:28-29

[230]   Deut 10:16

[231]   Luke 6:43-45

The Messiah and the resurrection

Bethany is a short distance east of Jerusalem, the village used to be known as Ananiah, one of the Bejaminite settlements around the city. It was where Lazarus and his sisters, Mary and Martha, close friends of Jesus, lived. They had first met when Martha opened her home to Jesus and his disciples, and while she was busy with preparing for them her sister, Mary, was sitting listening to what Jesus said. Martha then asked him if he cared that her sister had left her to do all the work by herself and that she needed her help. Jesus said to Martha, "Martha, Martha, you're worried and upset about many things, but only one thing is needed. Mary has chosen what is better and it'll not be taken from her."

Lazarus had become seriously ill and a message was sent to Jesus, who was on the east side of the River Jordan, simply saying, 'Lord, the one you love is sick.' When he received the message Jesus said to those with him that this sickness would not end in death but that it's for God's glory, so that his Son can be glorified through it. Jesus remained in that area for two more days.

"Let's go back to Judea," Jesus told his disciples.

"But Rabbi," they questioned, "not long ago you were almost stoned! Why go back there?"

"Are there not twelve hours of daylight?" Jesus reasoned. "A man who walks by day isn't going to stumble because he sees by this world's light. It's when he walks in the night that he stumbles because he has no light."

He then informed the disciples that, "Our friend Lazarus has fallen asleep and I'm going to wake him up."

"Lord, if he sleeps he'll get better."

"Lazarus is dead," Jesus plainly to them, "and for your sake I'm glad I wasn't there, so that you can believe; let's go to him."

Thomas then said, "We'll go as well so that we may die with him."

Many people when speaking of the dead will say that 'they are with the Lord,' or that they 'have entered glory.' However, Scripture never speaks of the soul going to another destination. This widespread teaching comes from Platonism and Gnosticism which greatly influenced the church of the 3rd and 4th century, as the church leadership then, and after, considered the writings of the philosophers as divine wisdom worthy of long and deep study. It was believed by many of the church's leadership that pagan Greek logic and Christian scholastic theology shared the same premises and were not really opposed to each other.[232]

The teaching that our soul is immortal comes from the same source. It is our spirit or mind that God retains at our death until the day of the resurrection when Christians will appear as immortal spiritual beings with the Messiah as he returns in glory to earth. Scripture is silent about any intermediate conscious state between physical death and the resurrection apart from how both Jesus and Paul term it; as a sleep. Lazarus was dead but Jesus called it a sleep, as Paul does in his letters as well as David, Daniel, Isaiah, and in the

---

[232]   See 'Aberlard' by M.T. Clancy, page 116.

book of Acts.[233] Moses wrote in one of his prayers, 'You sweep men away in the sleep of death.'

When Paul had to testify before the Sanhedrin, after being arrested for his own safety by the Roman authorities, he noticed that there were both Sadducees and Pharisees ready to accuse him so he raised his voice and said, "My brothers, I am a Pharisee, the son of a Pharisee. I stand on trial because of my hope in the resurrection of the dead." As soon as he said this a dispute broke out between the Pharisees and the Sadducees which set them against each other because, as Paul well knew, the Sadducees did not believe in a resurrection and angels and spirits, while the Pharisees did believe in them.[234]

The subject of going or not going to heaven never came up because Paul's hope, as well as many others, was the resurrection; Paul had preached the good news of Jesus and the resurrection,[235]not about going to heaven. Going to heaven is tied in with having an immortal soul, but as the soul is the person themselves, and mortal, the question of where do we go after death should be changed to what Paul said, "I want to know Christ and the power of his resurrection and the fellowship of sharing in his sufferings, becoming like him in his death, and so, somehow, to attain to the resurrection of the dead."[236]It's not where but what. The event is the resurrection and not the going to another place. When Paul said that he desired to depart and be with Christ, he knew that after death his next conscious moment would be his resurrection, irrespective of how long he had been dead.

Martha heard that Jesus was near Bethany and so she went out to meet him. By that time Lazarus had been in the tomb for four days,

---

233   See Psa 13:3, Dan 12:2, Isa 57:2, Acts 13:36, as well as 1 Cor 11:30, 15:6,18,20,51. 1 Thes 4:13-15. Psa 90:5.

234   Acts 23:6-8

235   Acts 17:18

236   Phil 3:10-11

and many Jews had come to comfort Martha and Mary in their loss as Jerusalem was less than two miles away.

Martha said to Jesus, "Lord, if you had been here my brother wouldn't have died, but I know that even now God will give you whatever you ask."

"Your brother will rise again," Jesus assured her.

"I know that he'll rise again in the resurrection at the last day," Martha affirmed.

"I am the resurrection and the life. Anyone who believes in me will live even though they die, and whoever lives and believes in me will never die. Do you believe this?"

"Yes Lord." Martha swallowed and held back her tears. "I believe that you are the Messiah, the Son of God, who was to come into the world."

Martha returned to Mary at their home and told her privately, "The Teacher is here and he's asking for you." Mary got up quickly and went to him as he was still just outside the village. When those who were there to comfort the sisters saw Mary leave the house they followed her thinking that she was going to mourn for her brother at his tomb.

As Mary drew close to Jesus her emotions welled up and she fell to the ground in front of him saying, "Lord, If only you'd been here my brother wouldn't have died."

Jesus looked at her as she cried along with the others who came with her and he became deeply moved with indignation because of the sorrow he saw around him, and he shook with the force of it, angry at death and the one who had the power of death – the devil.[237]

"Where have you laid him?" Jesus asked.

"Come and see, Lord," they answered.

Jesus walked with them as tears ran down his face. Those with him saw how moved he was and wondered why, as he could open the eyes of a blind man, he could not have saved Lazarus from dying.

Jesus, determined to oppose the enemy, strode to the tomb. The large stone that covered the entrance was before him, and he asked some men there to move the stone away, but Martha reminded him that by this time decay would have begun and that the smell would be bad.

"Didn't I tell you that if you believed you would see the glory of God?" Jesus reminded her of an earlier conversation they had when Lazarus was alive. The men then took the stone away and Jesus looked up and said, "Father, thank you that you've heard me – I know that you always hear me, but I said this for the benefit of the people standing here, so that they may believe that you sent me."

Jesus raised his voice so that all could hear him. "Lazarus, come out!"

Out of the darkness of the tomb the wrapped figure of Lazarus appeared, his face was covered by a cloth. "Release him," Jesus told the shocked and fearful onlookers, "and let him walk."[238]

Being released from death was the hope that Jesus taught to all who listened to him, including his critics. "I'm telling you the truth;

---

[237]   Heb 2:14

[238]   John 11:1-44

whoever hears my word and believes him who sent me has eternal life and will not be condemned because he has crossed over from death to life. A time is coming and now has come when the dead will hear the voice of the Son of God and those who hear will live.

"Don't be amazed at this because the time is coming when all who are in their graves will hear his voice and come out. Those who have done good will rise to live and those who have done evil will rise to be condemned."[239]

Paul spoke of that awakening as the blast of a trumpet in his letter to the Corinthians, and to the Thessalonians as 'a loud command, with the voice of the archangel and with the trumpet call of God, and the dead in Christ will rise first.'[240] However it's accomplished, the dead will be awakened.

When Jesus described conditions surrounding his return he spoke of the sign of the Son of Man that will appear in the sky, "and all the nations of the earth will mourn as they see the Son of Man coming on the clouds of the sky with power and great glory, and he will send his angels with a loud trumpet call and they will gather his elect from the four winds – from one end of the heavens to the other."[241]

Paul goes into some detail in writing about the resurrection. He makes the analogy of physical life, both human and non-human and of spiritual life. He speaks of the incredible diversity in nature and how there is diversity in heavenly things as well. He moves to a picture of planting noting that what is planted is not the same when it breaks through the soil; the seed becomes wheat or corn, or plants and trees – whatever the seed was, it now becomes something else.[242]

---

[239]   John 5:24-29

[240]   1Cor 15:52, 1 Thes 4:16

[241]   Matt 24:30-31

[242]   1Cor 15:35-49

This is how it will be in the resurrection: we are mortal; we will be raised immortal; we are weak; we will be raised powerful; we are corruptible; we will be raised incorruptible. As the stars differ in the intensity of their light so there will be differences in the resurrection. The first man Adam was of the earth and just as we are like him we will, in the resurrection, be like the man from heaven.

Jesus was with Peter, James and John on a high hill by themselves. They were there to pray and as Jesus was praying everything changed. For a very short time the disciples experienced the future. What they saw was Jesus shining like the sun and brighter than anything they had ever seen before. Two other individuals came into view talking with Jesus; listening to the conversation they discovered that one was Elijah and the other Moses. Jesus was talking to these important historic individuals about what was to happen to him in Jerusalem and his departure from earth. As this unique conversation was going on the disciples felt drowsy, but as they watched this glorious meeting they became more alert.

As Moses and Elijah were taking their leave of Jesus Peter blurted out, "Master, it's good for us to be here." He didn't really know what he was saying. "Let's put up three tents, one for each of you." While he was suggesting some sort of a mini Feast of Tabernacles when booths made from leafy branches would be erected, a cloud appeared and covered them. Now they experienced fear of the unknown and their apprehension grew when they heard a voice coming from inside the cloud.

The disciples on hearing this voice were terrified. "This is my Son, whom I love; I am delighted with him. Listen to him." This was too much for them and they fell to the ground. Jesus came over to them, "Get up; don't be afraid." They opened their eyes and saw Jesus looking just as he was before he changed.

As they came down from the hill Jesus ordered them not to tell anyone about the vision they had seen until the Son of Man was raised from the dead. The three disciples kept the matter to themselves but they didn't understand what 'rising from the dead' meant.

This vision was a preview of the time after the return of Jesus where those who belonged to him would be with him talking, discussing and implementing his kingdom here on earth. When Moses died on Mount Nebo the thousands of years that passed between that moment and the Messiah's return would seem as only a short sleep before he woke at the sound of a familiar voice, and then he would have been taken to meet Jesus as he descended back to earth with all the others, like Elijah, who had been God's servants in this dark age.

Daniel wrote of the time when multitudes who sleep in the dust of the earth will awake, some to everlasting life, others (at the second resurrection[243]) to shame and everlasting contempt. Those who are wise will shine like the brightness of the heavens, and those who lead many to righteousness like the stars forever and ever.[244]

---

[243]   Rev 20:5

[244]   Dan 12:2-3

The Messiah and judgment

It took a vision from God to enable Peter to enter the house of a Gentile. When he arrived in Caesarea and walked into the house he saw that many others had been invited to be there to listen to him. Peter had travelled over thirty miles in answer to this invitation to come and speak to a Roman citizen.

Looking round at this large gathering Peter said to them, "You are well aware that it is against our law for a Jew to associate with a Gentile or visit him but God has shown me that I should not call any man impure or unclean. So when I was sent for I came without raising any objection. May I ask why you sent for me?"

The man who had sent for Peter was Cornelius, a centurion in what was known as the Italian Regiment. Both he and his family were God-fearing and devout. He gave generously to those in need and prayed to God regularly. About three in the afternoon, four days before this historic meeting, he had a vision in which an angel in shining clothes said to him, "Your prayers and gifts to the poor have come up as a memorial offering before God. Send men now to Joppa to bring back a man named Peter. He's staying with Simon the tanner, whose house is by the sea."

Cornelius explained to Peter what had happened. "So I sent for you immediately and it was good of you to come. Now we're all here in the presence of God to listen to everything the Lord has commanded you to tell us."

"I now realise," Peter began, "how true it is that God doesn't show favouritism but accepts people from every nation who fear him and do what is right. You know the message God sent to the people of Israel – the good news of peace through Jesus the Messiah who is Lord of all. You also know what has happened throughout Judea beginning in Galilee after the baptism that John preached and how God anointed Jesus of Nazareth with the Holy Spirit and power. He went around doing good and healing all who were under the power of the devil, because God was with him.

"We are witnesses of everything he did in the country of the Jews and in Jerusalem. They killed him by hanging him on a tree, but God raised him from the dead on the third day and caused him to be seen, not by everyone but by those already chosen – those who ate and drank with him after he rose from the dead. He commanded us to preach to the people and to testify that he is the one whom God appointed as judge of the living and the dead. All the prophets speak about him saying that all who believe in him receive forgiveness for their sins through his name."

As Peter was finishing the Holy Spirit came on all who were listening. Those who had come with Peter were astonished that the gift of the Holy Spirit had been poured out even on the Gentiles because they heard them speaking in different languages and praising God.

"Can anyone prevent these people from being baptised?" Peter said, "They've received the Holy Spirit just as we have." They were then baptised in the name of Jesus the Messiah. Peter, at their request, then stayed there for a few days.[245]

Jesus is the judge of the living and the dead.

---

[245]   Acts 10

151

Paul was by himself in Athens, and as he walked among the temples and idols that filled this famous city he became distressed at what he saw. He entered the synagogue and reasoned with the Jews and God-fearing Greeks and each day he talked to those in the market area. One day a group of Epicurean and stoic philosophers began to dispute with him.

"What's this babbler trying to say," they scoffed.

"He seems to be advocating foreign gods," others suggested. They said this because Paul was talking about Jesus and the resurrection. They took him and brought him to a meeting of the Areopagus, who were the guardians of the city's religion, morals and education,[246]where they asked him, "May we know what this new teaching is that you're presenting? You're bringing some strange ideas to our ears and we want to know what they mean."

Standing up Paul said to them, "Men of Athens, I see that in every way you're very religious because as I walked around and carefully looked at your objects of worship I found an altar with the inscription: TO THE UNKNOWN GOD. Now what you worship as something unknown I'm going to speak about.

"The God who made the world and everything in it is the Lord of heaven and earth and doesn't live in temples, and he isn't served by humans as if he needed anything because it's he who gives life and breath to all things. From one man he made every nation and he determined the times set for them and the exact places where they should live. God did this so that people would seek him and find him, though he is not far from each one of us. For in him we live and move and have our being, as some of your own poets have said, 'We are his offspring.'

---

[246]   John R.W. Stott, 'The Message of Acts' p.283

So since we are God's offspring we shouldn't think that the divine being is like gold or silver or stone – an image made by somebody's design and skill. In the past God overlooked such ignorance but now he commands all people everywhere to repent, because he has set a day when he will judge the world with justice by the man he's appointed. He's given proof of this to everyone by raising him from the dead."

When they heard about the resurrection of the dead some of them sneered but others said, "We want to hear you again on this subject." Paul then left the Council. A few men became followers of Paul and believed his message, among them was Dionysius, a member of the Areopagus, also a woman named Damaris, and a number of others.[247]

Jesus will judge the world with justice.

Jesus gave parables that underlined the inevitability of judgment:

"A man had a fig-tree planted in his vineyard and he went to look for fruit on it, but didn't find any, and so he said to the man who took care of his vineyard, 'for three years I've been coming to look for fruit on this fig-tree and haven't found any. Cut it down! Why should it use up the soil?'

"'Sir,' the man replied, 'leave it alone for one more year and I'll dig round it and fertilise it. If it bears fruit next year, good, if not, then cut it down.'"

One morning Jesus, on his way back into Jerusalem, saw a fig-tree that looked as if it would have fruit on it because of all its leaves, and being hungry he looked for some, even though it wasn't the season for figs, there should have been some small figs there. Finding no fruit on the tree he spoke to it, "may no-one ever eat fruit from you again." The disciples were there and heard what he said.

---

[247]   Acts 17:16-34

The next morning they saw that the fig-tree was withered from its roots. Outwardly the tree had looked as if there would be plenty of fruit on it. Between the cursing of the fig-tree and its withering Jesus had visited the most holy place in Jerusalem – the house of God, which was intended to be a house of prayer.

As he entered the temple courts where all were permitted to be because if they wanted to offer a sacrifice their money needed to be exchanged into the approved currency, for which there was a fee, as well as a temple tax, so that they could buy an animal or bird for the sacrifice. He saw all this money changing hands and heard the noise of people and animals jostling together and he knew what he was about to do because he had looked around at everything the day before.

Jesus, furious at what at what the temple area had become then drove out all who were buying and selling there. He overturned the tables of the money-changers and the benches of those selling doves saying, "It is written, 'My house will be called a house of prayer,'[248]but you are making it a 'den of robbers'."[249] "Get out of here!" he shouted at the dove sellers, "how dare you turn my Father's house into a market." His disciples were later to remember what the psalmist had written; 'I'm a stranger to my brothers, an alien to my own mother's sons; for zeal for your house consumes me and the insults of those who insult you fall on me.'[250]

Angrily the religious authorities demanded a miraculous sign so that they could see that he had the authority to clear the temple. "Destroy this temple," Jesus answered them, "and I'll raise it again in three days."

---

[248]   Isa 56:7

[249]   Jer 7:11

[250]   Psa 69:8-9

Believing him to be mad they replied, "It's taken forty-six years so far to build this temple, and you're going to raise it in three days?" To them he was becoming a dangerous charlatan who needed to be stopped.

The blind and the lame came to him at the temple and he healed them, but when the chief priests and the teachers of the law saw the wonderful things he did and the children shouting in the temple area, "Hosanna[251]to the Son of David," they were angry.

"Do you hear what these children are saying?" they demanded of him.

"Yes, have you never read, 'From the lips of children and infants you have ordained praise?'"[252]

Then he left them and went out of the city to Bethany where he spent the night. The religious authorities he had spoken to then began looking for a way to kill him because they feared him due to how much the people wanted to hear him teach.

What was happening in the temple was as barren as that fruitless fig-tree. The worship taught and acted out in that temple was just that, an act – a set of rituals that had no impact on the hearts of those who performed them – their religion was barren because it neglected the most important things – justice, mercy and faithfulness and because of their neglect they were set on a course for judgment.[253]

Jesus taught, "Don't judge, or you too will be judged, because in the same way as you judge others you'll be judged, and with the measure you use, it will be measured to you."[254]

---

[251]   A Hebrew expression meaning 'Save!' which became an exclamation of praise.

[252]   Psa 8:2

[253]   The city was destroyed in AD 70.

[254]   Matt 7:1-2, 1 Cor 4:4-5, 11:31-32

And Paul wrote to the Corinthians, 'My conscience is clear but that doesn't make me innocent. It's the Lord who judges me, so judge nothing before the appointed time; wait till the Lord comes. He will bring to light what is hidden in darkness and will expose the motives of what is in people's hearts. At that time each will receive their praise from God.'

Paul went on to write, 'If we judged ourselves we wouldn't come under judgment. When we're judged by the Lord we're being disciplined so that we will not be condemned with the world.'

Half way into the annual Feast of Tabernacles, which lasted for eight days, Jesus went into the temple courts to teach, and those there who heard him were amazed at the quality and authority of his teaching.

"How did this man get such learning without having studied?" they asked.

"My teaching isn't my own. It comes from him who sent me. If anyone chooses to do God's will they'll find out whether my teaching comes from God or whether I speak on my own. He who speaks on his own does so that they can gain honour for themselves, but he who works for the honour of the one who sent him is a man of truth: there is nothing false about him. Hasn't Moses given you the law? Yet not one of you keeps the law. Why are you trying to kill me?"

"You're demon-possessed – who's trying to kill you?" the crowd answered.

"I did one miracle[255]and you're all astonished and indignant, yet because Moses gave you circumcision – although it really came through Abraham – you circumcise a child on the Sabbath, and so if a child can be circumcised on the Sabbath, so that the law of Moses

---

[255]   The healing of an invalid at the pool. John 5: 1-15

isn't broken because it must be done on the eighth day, why are you angry with me for healing the whole man on the Sabbath?

"Stop judging by mere appearances and make a right judgment."[256]

Their judging of him was done with a condemning mind and it's that condemning attitude that Christians should not have. However, they are to use their critical faculties in evaluating and discerning between good and bad, truth and error.

The writer of Hebrews says, 'Man is destined to die once and after that to face judgment, and the Messiah was sacrificed once to take away the sins of many people, and he will appear a second time, not to bear sin, but to bring liberation to those who are waiting for him.'[257]

Peter writes to his readers, 'Dear friends, don't be surprised at the painful trial you're suffering, as though something strange were happening to you, but rejoice that you participate in the sufferings of the Messiah, so that you'll be overjoyed when his glory is revealed.

'If you're insulted because of the Messiah's name you're blessed because the Spirit of glory and of God rests on you. If you suffer, it shouldn't be for any kind of criminality. However, if you suffer as a Christian don't be ashamed, but praise God that you bear that name. Because it's time for judgment to begin with the family of God, and if it begins with us, what will the outcome be for those who don't obey the good news of God?'[258]

---

[256]   John 7:14-24

[257]   Heb 9:27-28

[258]   1 Peter 4:12-17

The Messiah and healing

The mission of the Messiah was marked by his preaching of the good news of the kingdom and the healings that covered all types of diseases; those suffering severe pain, epilepsy, deafness, blindness, disabilities and demon-possession.

Jesus was willing to arouse opposition from the religious authorities by healing on the Sabbath, which was forbidden, unless a person's life was in danger, because freeing someone from a burden, whatever its cause was justifiable no matter what day of the week it happened on, in fact the Sabbath itself with all its man-made restrictions had become a burden.

Even though Jesus healed on the Sabbath the people were tied to the enforced tradition that they were not to seek healing on that day and so we read of them coming to Jesus in large numbers in the evening as the sun set, as days were counted from sunset to sunset.[259]

Often when a demon-possessed person was close to Jesus the evil spirit in them protested at his presence. One such spirit shouted, "What do want with us, Jesus of Nazareth? Have you come to destroy us before the appointed time? I know who you are – the Holy One of God!"[260]

---

[259]   Gen 1:5b

[260]   Mark 1:24

"Be quiet!" Jesus sternly responded, "Come out of him!" The man shook and shrieked as the spirit left him. This man had been sitting with the other worshippers in the synagogue without anyone knowing his true condition, or what lived within him. In the world many are plagued with evil spirits that are destroying their lives by controlling their thoughts and motives to do what is evil. And all of us are touched by madness in hidden places[261]

Jesus wouldn't let the demons speak because they knew who he was.

A man suffering an acute skin disease came to Jesus, and on his knees begged him, if he were willing, to make him clean. Filled with compassion Jesus placed his hand on the man and said, "I am willing; be clean!" Immediately the disease was gone.

"Don't stop to tell anyone about what's happened. You go to the priest and show him what's been done for you and offer the sacrifices that Moses commanded for your cleansing, as a witness to them."[262]But the man ignored what Jesus said and went out telling everyone about his cure. Because of this unwanted publicity Jesus couldn't openly enter a town and so he remained in the countryside, yet the people still came to him from every district.

Just a few days later he quietly returned to his home town Capernaum, but very soon everyone knew where he was and the house he was in was filled with people inside and outside. He began teaching them when everyone became distracted by noise coming from above them when dust and lumps of clay began falling on them. Those in the room, including some Pharisees got up and moved to the sides of the room but Jesus, looking up as sunlight broke into the room, remained calm.

---

[261]   'The Last Asylum' Barbara Taylor. p 259

[262]   Deut 24:8, Lev 14:2

Men's voices could be heard as they tore away at the roof and as soon as the hole was large enough a mat was carefully lowered and with some help from those below it was laid on the floor. On the mat lay a paralysed man and when Jesus saw the length his friends had gone to in getting this person to him he said to the paralytic, "Son, your sins are forgiven." This shocked the religious leaders there who saw themselves as the 'separated ones' with the aim of keeping the nation faithful to God, but mostly to their traditions.

"Who does this man think he is talking like that? He's blaspheming! Who but God can forgive sins?"

Jesus knew what they were thinking and he said to them, "Why are you thinking these things? Is it easier to say to the paralytic, 'Your sins are forgiven,' or to say, 'Get up, take your mat and walk'? But that you may know that the Son of Man has authority on earth to forgive sins," he turned to the man on the mat, "I tell you, get up, take your mat and go home." In front of all of them the man rose to his feet picked up his mat and walked out. This amazed everyone and they praised God because of what they had seen with their own eyes.

Jesus and the disciples had just disembarked from their boat on the east coast of the Sea of Galilee, which was a largely Gentile area, when a man who saw Jesus from a distance ran towards him. This man was possessed by an evil spirit and nobody was able to restrain him. He lived among the tombs and in the hills crying out and cutting himself with stones.

When he got to Jesus he dropped to his knees and cried out, "What do you want with me, Jesus, Son of the Most High God? Swear to God that you'll not torture me!" He said this because Jesus had commanded the evil spirit to come out of the man.

"What's your name?" Jesus asked.

"Legion. My name is Legion, because we're many." He begged Jesus repeatedly not to send them out of the area. There was a large herd of pigs feeding on a hillside close to where they were and the demons begged Jesus to allow them to enter the pigs. As Jesus gave them permission the herd, which numbered about two thousand, began to stir and then attempting to escape this brutal alien intrusion they rushed down the steep bank into the lake where they all drowned.

This disaster was quickly reported to the owners and to many others also who came to see what had happened. When they arrived at where Jesus was they saw this man who formally was naked and uncontrollable now dressed and sitting down. He was now liberated from this army of demons, and when they saw him they were afraid. They requested Jesus to leave their region and so he prepared to get back into the boat but as he was about to embark the man who had been demon-possessed begged to go with him.

"No. It's better that you go home to your family and tell them how much the Lord has done for you and the mercy he has shown you." The man did as Jesus said and told his story in the Decapolis[263]and everyone who heard it was amazed.

A large crowd gathered round Jesus when he returned to the west side of the lake and Jairus, one of the synagogue rulers, came to Jesus and implored him to come and heal his twelve year old daughter who was close to death. So Jesus went with him to his home.

On the way there many people were packed tightly around Jesus and his disciples and that made the going slow. Amongst this jostling crowd was a woman who had a problem with bleeding on which she had spent all her money on doctors who had not been able to help her, and now her condition was getting worse. She had heard about the healings Jesus had done and believed that if she could only get close enough to touch his clothes then she would be healed. Working

---

[263]   The League of Ten Cities established by Pompey

her way through the densely moving crowd she managed to break through close enough to reach out and touch the moving figure at the centre of this growing crowd. As her fingers lightly brushed against his cloak, immediately her bleeding stopped and her suffering was ended.

Jesus stopped. Sensing power had gone out from him and he asked, "Who touched my clothes?"

"Look how many people are crowding round you," his confused disciples answered, "and you're asking 'Who touched me?'"

Jesus scanned the crowd looking at each person until the woman trembling with fear and knowing that she had been healed came towards him and falling at his feet told him what had happened to her.

"Daughter, your faith has healed you. Go in peace and be free from your suffering." As he was speaking some men from Jarius's house came and told him that his daughter had died and so there was no need for the teacher to come.

Jesus heard this and said to Jarius, "Don't be afraid – just believe."

He took Peter, James and John, and with Jarius they continued to his home. When they got there they heard wailing and crying and going in he said to them, "Why all this noise and crying? The child is asleep, not dead." But they sneered and laughed at him, and so he put all of them outside and with just the disciples and the girl's parents they went into the room where the girl lay.

"He took her hand and said, "Little girl, I say to you, get up," and straight away the girl stood up and walked around; everyone was completely astonished. Jesus gave strict orders not to let anyone know about this and advised them to give the girl something to eat.

Jesus, having travelled from the vicinity of Tyre and moving north through Sidon and then south to the Sea of Galilee and then into the region of the Decapolis[264]met a group of people who brought to him a man who was deaf and could only make unintelligible sounds, and they asked him to place his hand on the man.

Jesus took the man and moved away from the crowds and then he placed his fingers into the man's ears and with his saliva he touched the man's tongue. Looking upwards he deeply sighed and said, "Be opened," then the man's ears were opened and his tongue loosened enabling him to speak plainly.

Jesus commanded them not to tell anyone, but the more he did so, the more they kept talking about it because they were overwhelmed with amazement.

A similar healing took place at Bethsaida, on the north-east of the Sea of Galilee, and Peter's home town, when some people brought a blind man to Jesus and begged him to heal this man. Jesus took his hand and walked with him outside of the town. He put saliva on his eyes and placed his hands on him. Jesus asked, "Do you see anything?"

"I see people, but they look like trees walking around."

Once more Jesus placed his hands on the man's eyes. Then his eyes were opened and his sight was restored, as he now saw everything clearly. Jesus sent him home with the same message he had given others: "Keep it to yourself."

Jesus did not deliberately look for big crowds. Simon and some other disciples went looking for Jesus because he had left the house that they were staying in early that morning, while it was still dark,

---

[264]   Originally they were ten Greek cities. It is also a geographical term referring to the area mostly south and east of the Sea of Galilee.

so that he could pray privately. And when they found him they told him, "Everyone is looking for you!"

"Let's go somewhere else," Jesus replied, "so that I can preach there also, because that's why I've come."

When Jesus was accused of spending time with sinners he answered, "The Son of Man came to look for the lost and save them."[265] Another time he said to those with the same complaint, "It's not the healthy that need a doctor but the sick, because I've not come to call the righteous but sinners."[266]

After Peter, James and John had seen Jesus transformed into a glorious light-emanating figure who was heard talking to Moses and Elijah and had heard the voice of God telling them to listen to his Son, they returned from that high place and saw the other disciples with a large crowd around them and the religious leaders were arguing with them.

"What are you arguing with them about?" Jesus asked them.

"Teacher," one of those in the front of the crowd answered, "I came to you with my son who is possessed by a spirit that has robbed him of speech. Whenever it seizes him he's thrown to the ground and foams at the mouth, gnashes his teeth and becomes rigid – I asked your disciples to drive out the spirit but they couldn't."

"O unbelieving generation, how long will I stay with you and how long have I to put up with you? Bring the boy to me."

As they brought the boy to him the spirit in the boy saw Jesus and immediately threw the boy into a convulsion. Falling to the ground he rolled around foaming at the mouth.

---

[265]   Luke 19:10

[266]   Matt 9:12-13

"How long has he been like this," Jesus asked the boy's father.

"From childhood. It has often thrown him into fire or water to kill him, but, if you can do anything take pity on us and help us."

"'If you can'?" Everything is possible for the person who believes."

"I do believe," the boy's father quickly responded, "help me overcome my unbelief!"

Jesus saw that more people were running towards them and so he turned to the boy and said, "You deaf and mute spirit, I command you, come out of him and never enter him again."

The boy convulsed violently as the spirit shrieked. His body lay on the ground as if he were dead, which is what those who saw him said, but Jesus took him by the hand and lifted him to his feet. He then returned him to his father. After Jesus had gone back indoors, and away from the crowd, his disciples asked him privately why they couldn't drive the spirit out.

"It's because you have so little trust – your faith is weak and your anxieties work against you, and your doubt divided your faith. Your faith needs to be a real and practical reliance on the living God; with just a little of this faith 'you could move mountains."

Much later Paul was to use the same expression in talking of the pre-eminence of love over all other virtues, 'If I have the gift of prophecy and can fathom all mysteries and all knowledge, and if I have a faith that can move mountains, but have not love, I am nothing.'[267]

He returned to Cana in Galilee, where he had changed water into wine, and while he was there an official of the royal household went

---

[267]   1Cor 13:2

to see him because his son was close to death, and he begged Jesus to come and heal him. His son was at Capernaum which was about twenty miles away.

"You're always looking for signs and wonders," Jesus said to him, "and without them you'll never believe."

"Sir, please, come to where my son is – or he'll be dead soon," the official pleaded with him.

"Go back to him," Jesus said to the distressed father, "your son will live." The man believed Jesus and set off back to home. Before he had arrived back in Capernaum his servants came to him and told him that his son had recovered. He asked them what time the boy had recovered and they told him that the fever left him the day before at one o'clock in the afternoon. Thinking back the father realised that that was the exact time Jesus had said to him, 'Your son will live.' Because of this he and his entire household believed.

There were times when Jesus didn't want anyone to know where he and his disciples were as he had important things to teach them.[268] One time he asked his disciples to get away from the crowds and get some rest, so they went away in a boat to a solitary place but many who saw them leave and recognised who they were ran around the coast line to get to where Jesus was headed and they got there before he arrived.

When Jesus landed and saw this large group of people who had come from the towns along the coast standing there waiting for him he had compassion on them because they were like sheep without a shepherd, and so he began teaching them many things.[269]

---

268   Mark 9:30

269   Mark 6:31-34

The prophet Isaiah had written that all of us are like sheep stubbornly doing our own thing and foolishly going our own way.[270]

Jesus not only opened eyes so that the blind could see; he opened minds so that the spiritually blind could understand.

On the road to Emmaus he talked to two disciples about his death, while they did not realise who it was they were talking to. As he explained from Moses and all the prophets why the Messiah had to suffer they began to understand the Scriptures in a new way and their hearts warmed at the stranger's teaching. It was only after they had persuaded him to stay at their home and he took some bread, gave thanks, broke it and handed it to them that their eyes were opened and they recognised him. He then disappeared.

Later when he appeared to his disciples who were all in a locked room he said to them, after they'd recovered from the shock, "This is what I told you while I was still with you: Everything must be fulfilled that is written about me in the law of Moses, the Prophets and the Psalms. Then he opened their minds so that they could understand the Scriptures. He told them, "This is what is written: The Messiah will suffer and rise from the dead on the third day, and repentance and forgiveness of sins will be preached in his name to all nations, beginning at Jerusalem. You are witnesses of these things.[271]

In the highly symbolic language of the book of Revelation, John takes us in vision to an unknown time in the future...

'Then the angel showed me the river of life as clear as crystal flowing from the throne of God and of the Lamb down the middle of the great street of the city. On each side of the river stood the tree of life bearing twelve crops of fruit and yielding its fruit every month, and the leaves of the tree are for the healing of the nations.

---

[270]   Isa 53:6

[271]   Luke 24:13-48

No longer will there be any curse. The throne of God and of the Lamb will be in the city and his servants will serve him. They will see his face and his name will be on their foreheads. There will be no more night. They will not need the light of a lamp or the light of the sun because the Lord God will give them light and they will reign forever.'[272]

---

[272]   Rev 22:1-5

The Messiah's identity

Calling a religious person a fraud and a self-righteous hypocrite will definitely incur a backlash of hostility and while this is what Jesus experienced when he exposed the religious pretentions of the Pharisees as mere window-dressing, the public in general did want to hear him but among them there was disagreement and confusion as to who Jesus was – was he the real Messiah or just one of a long line of would-be Messiahs?

"Isn't this the man they're trying to kill?" asked a man who saw that Jesus was openly speaking in the temple precincts.

"Here he is and they're not saying a word to him. Perhaps the authorities have decided that he is the Messiah, but we know where this man comes from and when the real Messiah arrives no-one will know where he's from."

Jesus lifted his voice, "Yes, you know me, and you know where I'm from. I'm not here on my own but he who sent me is true. You don't know him but I know him because I'm from him and he sent me."

Those who were angered by what he said tried to seize him but were not able to because his time had not yet come, but there were many who heard him who put their trust in him and said, "When the Messiah comes will he do more miraculous signs than this man?"

These comments were noted by the Pharisees and they, with the backing of the chief priests, sent temple guards to arrest him.

"I am with you for only a short time and then I go to the one who sent me. You will look for me but you will not find me and where I am you cannot come."

"Where does he intend to go that we cannot find him?" one of the crowd asked. "Will he go to where our people live scattered among the Greeks and teach them? What did he mean when he said, 'You will look for me but you will not find me,' and 'where I am you cannot come'?"

On the last and greatest day of the Feast,[273] Jesus stood up and said in a loud voice, "If anyone is thirsty allow him to come to me and drink. Whoever believes in me, as the Scripture has said,[274]streams of living water will flow from within him."

The response from the people was mixed; "Surely he's the Prophet." and "He's the Messiah." but also, "How can the Messiah come from Galilee? Doesn't the Scripture say that the Messiah will come from David's family and from Bethlehem, the town where David lived?" People were divided because of Jesus and some of them wanted him to be arrested.

Finally the temple guards returned to the chief priests and Pharisees who asked them, "Why didn't you bring him in?"

"No-one ever spoke the way this man does." The guards replied.

---

[273]   The eighth day of the Feast of Tabernacles.

[274]   Possibly Isa 55:1-3. Jesus was talking of the Holy Spirit which was to be given.

"You mean he's deceived you also? have any of the rulers or of the Pharisees believed in him? No! But this mob that knows nothing of the law has a curse on them."

"Does our law condemn a man without first hearing him to find out what he's doing?" All eyes turned to Nicodemus who earlier had secretly visited Jesus at night.

"Are you from Galilee too? Look into it and you'll find that the Prophet doesn't come out of Galilee."

Caesarea Philippi was located in the south-western foothills of Mount Hermon, at one of the sources of the Jordan River. From ancient times it contained, within a cave among the high cliffs near the city, a shrine to Pan and the Greeks dedicated the spring to this god. Many rock-cut niches there held dedicatory statues of the nymphs and the area was named Paneas. Herod the Great built a temple there and dedicated it to Augustus and when his son Philip inherited this region he enlarged the city and renamed it Caesarea Philippi in honour of Caesar and himself. This centre of Greco-Roman civilisation controlled the surrounding region and was largely pagan.

Jesus and his disciples were in this region and he asked them, "Who do people say I am?"

"Some say John the Baptist, others say Elijah or Jeremiah, or one of the prophets."

"But what do you think? Who do you think I am?"

Simon Peter answered, "You're the Messiah, the Son of the living God."

"Congratulations, Simon son of Jonah, because this has been revealed to you, not by any other person, but by my Father in heaven.

I've named you Peter for a reason, because as your name means rock that rock will be the foundation of building the people of the Messiah and it will never die. I will give you the keys of the kingdom of God – a delegated authority – and whatever you permit on earth has already been permitted in heaven and whatever you don't permit hasn't been permitted in heaven."

Then he warned them not to tell anyone that he was the Messiah as their expectations of what the Messiah is to do will be greatly misunderstood because he must go to Jerusalem and suffer many things at the hands of the elders, chief priests and teachers of the law – there he must be killed and on the third day he will be raised to life."

Peter couldn't understand why Jesus spoke of failure rather than success so he took him away from the group and began to warn him of speaking so negatively, "Never Lord, listen to me, this disaster you talked about will never happen to you!"

Jesus faced Peter and so that the others could hear as well, he said, "Get behind me Satan! You're a rock to stumble over for me and your thinking doesn't come from God but is human, and is the mind of the enemy.

The Winter Feast

It was the 14th December and Jesus was walking through the covered colonnade named after Solomon which ran along the east side of the outer court of Herod's temple. It was the Feast of Dedication[275] also known as the Feast of Lights, and it lasted for eight days.

As he walked a group of men closed in on him and demanded that he plainly tell them if he were the Messiah or not.[276]

"I did tell you but you don't believe. The miracles I do in my Father's name speak for me but you don't believe because you're not my sheep. My sheep listen to my voice – I know them – and they follow me. I give them eternal life and they'll never perish. No-one can take them from me. My Father, who has given them to me, is greater than all and no-one can take them from him. I and the Father are one."

This was too much for them and as they were reaching for the nearest stones Jesus said to them, "I've shown you many great and beautiful miracles from the Father – for which of these do you stone me?"

---

[275]   The re-dedication of the temple (Hanukkah) established by Judas Maccabeus on 14th Dec. 165/4 BC.

[276]   John 10:24

"We're not stoning you for any of these but for blasphemy, because you, a mere man, claim to be God."

"Isn't it written in your Law, 'I have said you are gods'[277]If he called them 'gods'[278]to whom the word of God came, and the Scripture cannot be broken, what about the one whom the Father set apart as his very own and sent into the world? So why then do you accuse me of blasphemy because I said, 'I'm God's Son'? Don't believe me unless I do what my Father does, but if I do it, even though you don't believe me, believe the miracles, so that you can know and understand that the Father is in me and I in the Father."

Again they attempted to seize him but he escaped from them.

Jesus crossed back over the Jordan to the place where John had been baptising in the early days. He remained there and many people came to him saying, "Though John never performed a miraculous sign, all that John said about this man was true." And in that place many believed in Jesus.

---

[277]   Psalm 82:6

[278]   The nation of Israel and their unjust leaders

Why the Messiah had to die

After Lazarus was resurrected to physical life many people were putting their trust in Jesus and so the religious leadership decided that Lazarus must die as well as Jesus.

At a specially convened meeting of the Sanhedrin, the supreme court of the Jewish nation called by the chief priests and the Pharisees, it was said, "We've not been able to stop this growing enthusiasm for Jesus and as long as he keeps performing these miracles his support is going to grow. If we allow him to continue everyone is going to believe in him and then the Romans will come and take away everything we value including our nation itself."

Caiaphas, who had been high priest since AD 18, when he was appointed by the Roman prefect Valerius Gratus, spoke up, "You don't know the first thing! You need to realise that it's better for all of us that one man die for the people than the whole nation perish." From that day on they plotted to take his life.

Jesus no longer moved about in public, instead he withdrew to a region near the desert in a village called Ephraim.

When the time was getting close for the Passover many travelled to Jerusalem for their ceremonial washing before the feast. They hoped to see Jesus there and asked each other if they thought he would publicly show himself, because the chief priests and the Pharisees had issued orders that if anyone had any knowledge of where he was then they should report it to the authorities so that they could arrest him. Privately they agreed that Jesus shouldn't be put to death during the Feast in case it provoked a riot among the people.

Jesus came to Bethany six days before the Passover where a dinner in his honour was given by Lazarus and his sisters, Martha and Mary. Their father Simon was there as well. As they reclined around the low tables Mary brought in an alabaster container holding half a litre of pure nard, a very expensive perfume that was grown in India. She broke the top off the sculptured container and began to pour it onto the feet of Jesus and then with her loosened hair she wiped his feet, and the house was filled with the fragrance of the perfume.

Judas Iscariot objected, as did the other disciples, and said, "This perfume could have been sold and the money given to the poor – it's worth at least a year's wages!" Judas was a thief and didn't care about the poor. As the man in charge of the money his practice was to help himself to their funds.

"Why are you troubling this woman?" Jesus said, "She has done a beautiful thing to me. You'll always have the poor with you but you won't always have me. When she poured this perfume on me that had been saved for this moment she did it to prepare me for burial. Wherever this message is preached what she has just done will also be told, in memory of her."

Then Judas went to the chief priests and asked, "What are you willing to give me if I hand him over to you?" They were delighted and so they gave him thirty pieces of silver, and Judas waited for an opportunity to betray him.

The next day the word had spread quickly that Jesus was on his way to Jerusalem and they tore off branches from the palm trees[279]and went out to meet him.

When Jesus came to the Mount of Olives overlooking the Temple, he sent two of his disciples ahead to one of the city's suburbs to collect a colt that would be tied near a door. When they found the colt and untied it some people asked them what they were doing and they said to them, "The Lord needs it, and you'll get it back shortly." After getting permission to take it they brought it to Jesus and having placed some of their cloaks over it he sat on it and headed for the city. By now a huge crowd was lining the way and having joined him they now escorted him into the city – as would be the custom for a visiting king or emperor.[280]

The crowd's excitement was as if they were welcoming a liberator. "Victory now!" they shouted, and quoting the psalm, "O Lord, save us, O Lord, grant us success. Blessed is he who comes in the name of the Lord."[281] This joyous celebration was a fulfilment of what the prophet Zechariah wrote, 'Rejoice greatly, O daughter of Zion! Shout, daughter of Jerusalem! See, your king comes to you, righteous and having salvation, gentle and riding on a donkey, on a colt, the foal of a donkey.'[282] The Pharisees who grimly watched this noisy parade said "Look how the whole world has gone after him!"

The miracle worker was now publicly with them and the disciples joined their voices to the growing crowds who became a sea of praise while the Pharisees were indignant at such unrestrained and

---

[279]   Lev 23:40 Palm fronds were used in times of celebration as well as the fruit from the trees and their leafy branches.

[280]   The Greek word for such an occasion is *Parousia*.

[281]   Psa 118:25-26

[282]   Zec 9:9

triumphant rejoicing. "Teacher, calm your disciples – order them to stop!" They appealed to Jesus.

"I tell you that if they kept quiet the stones will start shouting!"

As he approached the city and looked at it he began to cry and said, "If you, even you, had only known today what would bring you peace, but it's hidden from you and you can't see it. The days will come when your enemies will build an embankment against you and encircle you and hem you in on every side. They will destroy you and your families within this city and they won't leave one stone on another because you didn't recognise the time of God's coming to you."

As he continued to teach at the temple courts, a mixed collection of the religious hierarchy questioned him on what authority he had to teach and who gave that authority to him.

"I will also ask you a question," Jesus replied, "Tell me, John's baptism, was it from heaven or from men?"

They looked at each other and weighed up their options. "If we say, 'From heaven,' he'll ask, 'Why didn't you believe him?' But if we say, 'From men', all the people will stone us, because they're sure that John was a prophet."

"We can't say as we don't know where it was from," they gambled that this compromise of an answer would be enough to get them off the hook.

"Neither will I tell you by what authority I'm doing these things." Jesus told them.

Keeping a close watch on him, they sent men undercover attempting to trip him up by saying something that would enable them to hand him over to the authority of the governor.

"Teacher," one of these agents asked, "we know that you speak and teach what is right and that you don't show partiality but teach the way of God in accordance with the truth. Is it right for us to pay taxes to Caesar or not?"

This duplicity was clear to Jesus and so he said to him, "Show me a denarius," someone helpfully handed him one. Looking at the coin he gave it back and asked, "Whose portrait and inscription are on it?"

"Caesar's" they answered.

"Then give to Caesar what belongs to Caesar and to God what belongs to God."

They were unable to trap him in what he said there in public and taken back by his answer they became silent.

The Messiah's time has come

Philip, who was from Bethsaida in Galilee, was approached by some Greeks who wanted to meet Jesus, he told Andrew and they both went and told Jesus of the Greek's request.

"The hour has come for the Son of Man to be glorified," Jesus said to his disciples. "I'm telling you the truth, unless a grain of wheat falls to the ground and dies it remains only a single seed, but if it dies it produces many seeds. Those people who love their life will lose it, while those who hate their life in this world will keep it forever. Whoever serves me must follow me and where I am my servant will be there also. My Father will honour the one who serves me.

"Now my heart is troubled and what shall I say? 'Father, save me from this hour'? No, it was for this very reason I came to this hour. Father, glorify your name!"

A voice like thunder came from above, "I've glorified it and will glorify it again." Those around him heard the voice and some said that an angel had spoken to him.

"This voice was for your benefit, not mine," Jesus said, "now is the time for judgment on this world for what it's about to do and the prince of this world – who leads the whole world astray – will be defeated, and I, when I'm lifted up from the earth, will draw all, without distinction of race, from all nations to me."

"We've heard from the law that the Messiah will remain forever," Jesus was asked. "So how can you say, 'The Son of Man must be lifted up'? Who is this 'Son of Man'?"

"You're going to have the light just a little while longer. Walk while you have the light before darkness overtakes you. The man who walks in the dark doesn't know where he's going so put your trust in the light while you have it – if you do you'll become sons of light."

After seeing the great miracles that Jesus did they still wouldn't believe in him. This stubborn and hardhearted attitude was a fulfilment of what Isaiah had written. 'Lord, who has believed our message and to whom has the arm of the Lord been revealed?'[283]They couldn't believe because as Isaiah was instructed to say to the people, 'Be ever learning but never understanding; be ever seeing but never perceiving. Make the heart of this people calloused; make their ears dull and close their eyes. Otherwise they might see with their eyes, hear with their ears, understand with their hearts, and turn and be healed.'[284]

Isaiah wrote this because he saw Jesus' glory and wrote about him.

At the same time many even among the leaders believed in him but because of the Pharisees they wouldn't confess their faith for fear that they would be put out of the synagogue. They loved praise from men more than praise from God.

"When a person believes in me he doesn't believe in me only but in the one who sent me and when he looks at me he sees the one who sent me. I've come into the world as a light so that no-one who believes in me should stay in darkness. As for the person who hears my words but doesn't keep them I don't judge them because I didn't come to judge the world but to save it. There is a judge for

---

[283]   Isa 53:1

[284]   Isa 6:9-10

the one who rejects me and doesn't accept my words, and that is the words which I spoke – that's what will condemn them at the last day, because I didn't speak of my own accord, but the Father who sent me commanded me what to say and how to say it. I know that his command leads to eternal life. So whatever I say is just what the Father has told me to say."

The Messiah's last Passover

The Feast of Unleavened Bread is in the first month in the sacred calendar Nisan, from the 15th to the 21st, but Passover day begins on the evening of the 14th of Nisan. The first day of unleavened bread is the first of the annual holy days which is a Sabbath of rest separate from the weekly Sabbath. The last day of unleavened bread is also a Sabbath. There are seven in all of these special days that Israel was commanded to keep. Passover was seen as part of the days of unleavened bread although it came a day before that first annual Sabbath.

On the day that Jesus chose to eat his last Passover meal with his disciples they asked him where he wanted them to go and make the necessary preparations so that they could eat the Passover.

He sent two of them into the city where they would meet a man carrying a jug of water. They were to follow him and say to the owner of the house he enters, 'The Teacher asks: Where is my guest room where I may eat the Passover with my disciples?' He will show them a large furnished upper room where they are to make preparations for all of them. This they did.

When evening came Jesus and the disciples reclined at the table, and he said to them, "I have eagerly desired to eat this Passover with you before I suffer – I will not eat it again until it finds fulfilment in the kingdom of God." While they were eating he said, "The truth is that one of you who is eating with us will betray me." He appeared troubled and saddened at having to say this.

One by one they protested their innocence. "It is one of the twelve," Jesus replied, "one who dips bread into the bowl with me. The Son of man will go just as it's written about him, but disaster will come to that man who betrays the Son of Man! It would be better for him for him if he had not been born."

His disciples stared at each other at a loss to know which of them he meant. As John was reclining next to Jesus Peter looked over to him and suggested by his expression that he should ask Jesus which one of them he means.

"Lord, who is it?" John asked as he was leaning against him.

"It's the one to whom I will give this piece of bread when I've dipped it into the dish." Dipping the piece of bread he gave it to Judas Iscariot and as soon as he took the bread Satan entered him.

"What you're about to do, do quickly," Jesus told him, but no-one at the meal understood why Jesus said this to him. Since Judas had charge of the money some thought he was being told to buy what was needed for the Feast or to give something to the poor. As soon as Judas had taken the bread he went out, and it was dark.

When he was gone Jesus said, "Now is the Son of Man glorified and God is glorified in him." Jesus then addressed the disciples as his dear children, even though he was in his early thirties, "I will be with you only a little longer – you'll look for me and just as I told those outside, so I now tell you – where I'm going, you cannot come.

"I'm giving you a new command: Love one another. Just as I've loved you so you must love one another, and by this everyone will know that you are my disciples."

"Lord, where are you going?" Peter asked him.

"Where I'm going you cannot follow, but you will follow later."

"Lord. Why can't I follow you now? I'll lay down my life for you." The others said the same, but Jesus told them, "You will all fall away because it's written, 'I will strike the shepherd and the sheep will be scattered.'[285]"Even if all fall away I will not," Peter insisted.

"Will you really lay down your life for me? I'm telling you the truth, before the cock crows you'll disown me three times."

While they were eating Jesus took bread gave thanks and broke it. He then gave it to his disciples and said, "Take and eat; this is my body given for you; do this in remembrance of me."

Then he took the cup containing wine and offered it to them. "All of you drink from it – this is my blood of the new covenant which is poured out for many for the forgiveness of sins. I'll not drink of this fruit of the vine from now until the day when I drink it with you in my Father's kingdom."[286]

Jesus asked them, "When I sent you without purse, bag or sandals, did you lack anything?"

"Nothing," they answered.

"But now if you have a purse, take it, and also a bag, and if you don't have a sword sell your cloak and buy one because it's written, 'and he was numbered with the transgressors',[287]and this

---

[285]   Zec 13:7

[286]   The communion is taken in remembrance of him, 1 Cor 11:24-25. It is also a participation in him, 1 Cor 10:6. And it is a proclamation of his death until he comes, 1 Cor 11:26.

[287]   Isa 53:12

must be fulfilled in me, yes, what is written about me is reaching its fulfilment."

"See, Lord, here are two swords."

"They'll be enough."

A little later he told them, "You heard me say, 'I'm going away and I'm coming back to you.' If you loved me you would be glad that I'm going to the Father, because the Father is greater than me. I've told you now, before it happens, so that when it does happen you'll believe. I'll not speak with you much longer because the prince of this world is coming; he has no hold over me but the world must learn that I love the Father and that I do exactly what my Father has commanded me. It's time to go – let's leave."

Arrest and trial

When Jesus had finished praying for himself, his disciples and for those who would later believe, he left with his disciples and crossed the Kidron Valley, and they came to an olive grove on the slopes of the Mount of Olives which they entered. Judas knew of this place because Jesus had often met there with his disciples and so he led a large group of soldiers and temple police who were armed and carrying torches.

Judas had arranged a signal with them that the one he kisses is the man they wanted and as he approached Jesus to kiss him Jesus asked him, "Judas, are you betraying the Son of Man with a kiss?" He then kissed Jesus after calling him Rabbi.

Knowing all that was going to happen to him Jesus turned to face the soldiers and officials and asked them, "Who is it you want?" They didn't see a fugitive ready to run but a commanding figure who spoke without fear.

"Jesus of Nazareth," they replied.

"I am the man," and as he said these words there was a moment when terror entered them and the ones in front fell back, bumping into those behind them, again Jesus, fully in control, asked, "Who is it you want?"

"Jesus of Nazareth," they repeated as they regained their footing.

"I told you that it's me, and as you're looking for me then let these men go." Then Peter drew his sword and hit Malchus, the high priest's servant, cutting his right ear off.

"Put your sword away!" Jesus ordered Peter. "Shall I refuse to drink the cup the Father has given me?" Jesus touched the man's ear and healed him. "Am I leading a rebellion that you've come with swords and clubs? Every day I was with you in the temple courts and you didn't lay a hand on me, but this is your hour – when darkness reigns."

Then his disciples quickly left him and ran for their lives. A young man, wearing nothing but a linen garment was following Jesus, and when they tried to hold him he ran away naked leaving his garment behind.

Jesus was securely tied and taken to Annas, the former high priest and father-in-law to Caiaphas. After the disciples had quickly exited from the olive grove two of them, Peter and John, returned and followed Jesus and his armed guard to the home of Annas. Because John had had a business connection with the high priest he was allowed in but Peter had to wait outside at the door. John returned to the front door and spoke to the girl who checked who came in and Peter was able to enter.

But the girl was suspicious of Peter and confronted him, "You're not one of his disciples, are you?"

"I'm not," Peter stated.

Being a cold night, people were standing round a fire to keep warm and Peter joined them and warmed himself. By this time Annas had begun questioning Jesus about his teaching and his disciples. Jesus answered, "I've spoken openly to the world and always taught in synagogues or at the temple where all the people come together.

I said nothing in secret so instead of questioning me you should ask those who heard me – they know what I said."

One of the officials standing close to Jesus was angered by what he said and struck him in the face. "Is this the way you answer the high priest?" he demanded.

"If I said something wrong say what was wrong, but if I spoke the truth why did you hit me?"

Then Annas sent him, still bound, to Caiaphas, the reigning high priest, who was in another part of the building, having assembled the ruling teachers of the law and the elders.

As Peter stood warming himself, another girl saw him and said to the others there, "This man was with Jesus of Nazareth."

"I swear I don't know the man!" Peter said. A short while later a group of those at the fire went to Peter and said, "I'm sure that you're one of them because you've got a Galilean accent." Peter began using bad language and insisting that he really didn't know the man and at that moment a cock began to crow. Jesus turned and looked straight at Peter and he remembered what Jesus had said to him, and he went outside and wept bitterly.

The whole Sanhedrin was looking for evidence against Jesus so that they could put him to death, but they did not find any even though many false witnesses came forward. Finally two came forward and said, "This man said that he was able to destroy the temple of God and rebuild it in three days." Yet even then their testimonies did not agree.

"Aren't you going to answer?" The high priest asked Jesus. "These men are bringing serious charges against you." But he remained silent and gave no answer. Frustrated at getting no reply Caiaphas stood up and raising his voice he said to Jesus, "I charge you under oath by the living God to tell us if you are the Messiah, the Son of God!"

"I am, and you will see the son of Man at the right hand of the mighty One and coming on the clouds of heaven."

"Why do we need any more witnesses?" the high priest cried as he tore his clothes.[288]"You've heard the blasphemy, what do you think?"

"He's worthy of death," they shouted. Then the guards spat in his face and hit him with their fists while others slapped him. He was insulted and blindfolded as they taunted him with demands to tell them who hit him.

At daybreak the supreme council met again and formally agreed to the decision to put Jesus to death. The bound him and prepared to hand him over to Pilate, the governor.

Judas realised that Jesus was condemned and he was gripped by remorse and so he returned the thirty silver coins to the chief priests and the elders. "I've sinned because I've betrayed innocent blood."

"What's that to us? That's your business – not ours."

Judas threw the money into the temple and left. The chief priests then picked up the coins and said, "It's against the law to put this money into the treasury since it is blood money." They decided to use the money to buy the potter's field as a burial place for foreigners.

Judas went down into the Valley of Hinnom and hanged himself but his body fell and his stomach was torn open. That is why it has been called the Field of Blood to this day. The words of the prophet were fulfilled: "they took the thirty silver coins, the price set on him

---

[288]   A traditional show of emotion on hearing what he considered blasphemy.

by the people of Israel and they used them to buy the potter's field, as the Lord commanded me."[289]

Jesus was taken to the Antonia fortress, which was the headquarters of the Roman military governor. But they didn't enter the building due to their ceremonial cleanness which would be compromised if they entered a building which contained Gentiles, and so Pilate came out to them.

"What charges are you bringing against this man?" Pilate asked them.

"If he wasn't a criminal we wouldn't have handed him over to you."

"You take him and judge him by your own law."

"But we've no right to execute anyone."

Pilate went back inside and summoned Jesus to answer his questions; "Are you the king of the Jews?"

"Is that your own idea or did others talk to you about me?"

Am I a Jew? It was your own people and your chief priests who handed you over to me – what is it you've done?"

"My kingdom is not of this world. If it were, my servants would fight to prevent my arrest, but my kingdom is from somewhere else."

"You are a king then?"

---

[289]   Jer 19:1-13, Zech 11: 12-13, Jer 32:6-9. Matthew has conflated quotations from both writers, as Mark does in 1:2-3 which conflates Malachi and Isaiah and is ascribed to Isaiah. See Michael Green's Matthew, p288.

"You're right in saying I am a king. In fact it was for this reason I was born, and I came into the world so that I could testify to the truth. Everyone on the side of truth listens to me."

"What's truth?" Pilate then went out to where the accusers were impatiently waiting and said to them, "I find no basis for a charge against him – but it's your custom for me to release to you one prisoner at the time of the Passover. Do you want me to release this 'king of the Jews'?"

"No, not him!" they shouted back, "Give us Barabbas!"[290]Barabbas had been arrested as an insurgent as were the two other condemned men. Pilate was told that Jesus began his teaching in Galilee and on hearing this he asked if he were a Galilean and when he learned that he was and that Herod had jurisdiction over that area Pilate sent Jesus to Herod who happened to be in Jerusalem at that time.

When Herod saw Jesus he was very pleased because he had been waiting a long time to see him and he hoped that Jesus would perform some miracle for him. He asked Jesus many questions but Jesus did not answer him even though the chief priests and the teachers of the law were there aggressively accusing him. Herod and his soldiers then ridiculed and mocked him, dressing him in an elegant robe and then they sent him back to Pilate. On that day relations between Herod and Pilate improved.

Pilate addressed Jesus' accusers, "You brought me this man as one who was inciting the people to rebellion, but I've examined him in your presence and have found no basis for your charges against him – neither has Herod because he sent him back to us – as you can see! He's done nothing to deserve death so I'll punish him and then release him."

---

[290]   Barabbas means 'son of Abba' or 'son of the father' Barabbas must have had his own name and some ancient manuscripts tell us that it was the common name of Jesus – Jesus son of the father!

Then Pilate took Jesus and had him flogged. While Pilate sat on the judges seat his wife[291] sent him a message; 'Don't have anything to do with this innocent man because I've suffered a great deal today in a dream because of him.'

The soldiers led Jesus away into the Praetorium and called together the whole company who provided a mock guard of honour. They looked on the Jews as a despised subject people for whom they would have no sympathy. Their intention was to dress him as a king and they used what was at hand. They stripped him and put a scarlet robe on him and then twisted a crown of thorns and set it on his head, and in his right hand they put a staff. With this crude mockery of kingship completed, they knelt in front of him hailing the newly crowned king of the Jews.

Tiring of this they spat on him and took the staff and repeatedly hit him on his head. When they finished mocking him they took him back to Pilate who presented him to the crowd. "Look at the man!" he said, "I want you to know that I find no basis for a charge against him." As soon as the chief priests and officials saw him they shouted, "Crucify! Crucify!"

"You take him and crucify him. As for me, I find no basis for a charge against him."

"We have a law," they answered, "and according to that law he must die because he claimed to be the Son of God."

Pilate was even more uneasy when he heard that charge – could he really be who he claimed to be? He went back inside and asked Jesus, "Where do you come from?" But Jesus didn't answer. "Do you refuse to answer me? Don't you realise I've the power to free you, or to crucify you."

---

[291]   Claudia Procula, the illegitimate daughter of Claudia, Tiberius's third wife – grand-daughter of Augustus.

"You'd have no power over me if it were not given to you from above, so the one who handed me over to you is guilty of a greater sin."

From then on Pilate tried to set Jesus free, but the crowd kept baying for his blood. "If you let this man go," they shouted, "you're no friend of Caesar. Anyone who claims to be a king opposes Caesar."

Pilate realised he was getting nowhere and the crowd were becoming uncontrollable. He sat on the judge's seat and said once more, "Here is your king, shall I crucify your king?"

"We have no king but Caesar," they responded.

"I'm innocent of this man's blood," Pilate told them, "It's your responsibility!"

"Let his blood be on us and on our children!" They answered.

Pilate then washed his hands and released Barabbas and handed Jesus over to be crucified.

The Messiah crucified

In preparation for the crucifixion Jesus was scourged, as were the other two that would be executed; it was standard practice. This punishment was used as a preliminary to execution and was sometimes fatal by itself. It was inflicted by a whip of several thongs, each of which was loaded with pieces of bone or metal. It was possible to flay a person to the bone with it.

The three condemned men were taken out through one of the city gates each carrying their cross-piece[292]and hanging from their necks a placard with their crime written on it. The two with Jesus had 'insurgent' on theirs but the writing on the sign Jesus carried was ordered by Pilate himself. It read: JESUS OF NAZARETH THE KING OF THE JEWS. It was written in Aramaic, Latin and Greek. When the Jewish authorities saw it they petitioned Pilate to change it to 'This man claimed to be king of the Jews,' but Pilate told them, "What I've written will not be changed."

The cross beam that Jesus was carrying became too heavy for him and a man in the crowd was pressed into carrying it for him. His name was Simon, who just happened to be there that day, and he was from Cyrene, on the coast of eastern Libya.

---

[292]   Films always show the two criminals carrying the cross-piece but Jesus carrying the whole cross. This is a case of faithfulness to the imagery of the stations of the cross overriding historical fact.

Many people were following Jesus to his execution, including women who cried for him. He faced these women and said, "Daughters of Jerusalem, don't cry for me – cry for yourselves and your children because the time will come when you'll say, 'happy are the women without children and who have never nursed them,'" he then quoted the prophet Hosea, "They will say to the mountains, 'Cover us!" and to the hills, "Fall on us!"[293] And he ended by speaking of men doing these things when the tree is green but what, he asked, will they do when it's dry. This could have meant; "If you think this is a tragic and sad time there is much worse coming."

They arrived at the place of the skull (which in Aramaic is called Golgotha). This execution area was quite close to one of the city gates and unavoidable to the heavy traffic that would pass by. The Romans always used a public place because of its deterrent value. The upright stakes for the cross-pieces to be attached to were already there. When the soldiers had finished nailing the three, usually through the forearms or wrists and one nail through both ankles, they took the clothes Jesus had been wearing, (the crucified men were now naked) and divided them into four parts because there were four soldiers in the execution squad, but the remaining undergarment was seamless, woven in one piece from top to bottom.

"Let's not tear it. We'll decide by lot who'll get it." The soldiers agreed.

It was about 9am.

A thousand years before, King David had written, 'Dogs have surrounded me, a band of evil men has encircled me, they have pierced my hands and my feet. I can count all my bones; people stare and gloat over me. They divide my garments among them and cast lots for my clothing.'[294]

---

[293]   Hos 10:8

[294]   Psa 22:16-18

As this was going on Jesus said, "Father, forgive them, because they don't know what they're doing." As well as the normal human traffic at that time there were also many who just came to watch and were standing at this busy intersection staring at these three men who were slowly dying in pain while others slowly walked past directing their insults particularly at Jesus, shaking their heads in mock sorrow and saying, "So, you're going to destroy the temple and build it in three days, are you?" Most of the mockery was coming from the religious leaders. "He saved others but he can't save himself – let's see if this Messiah – this King of Israel – will come down from the cross – if we see that we'll believe! He trusts in God; let's see God rescue him, if he wants him!

The soldiers also came up close and mocked him and one of them, who had become, for some unknown reason, full of hostility towards Jesus spat out, "If you're the King of the Jews save yourself." Like others his hate and contempt for this condemned man expressed itself in obscenities and ridicule. One of the criminals hanging there was also hurling his insults at Jesus saying, "Aren't you the Messiah? Well, save yourself and us as well!" The other man hanging from the cross told him to keep quiet, "Don't you fear God since you're under the same sentence? We're punished justly because we're getting what we deserve but this man has done nothing wrong." He turned his head to look at Jesus, "Jesus, remember me when you come into your kingdom."

Jesus looked at him, "Today, as we hang here together dying, I can tell you that you will be with me in paradise."[295]

At midday darkness came over all the land and God's judgment on sin was near. It was to last for three hours. All the sins of the world were about to be paid for.[296]Not far from the cross of Jesus a group

---

[295]   Isa 51:3 As the garden of Eden was.

[296]   1 John 2:2

of women stood, including his mother and aunt, and with them was the disciple John. When Jesus saw them he said, "Dear woman, here is your son," and to John he said, "Here is your mother." From then on John took her into his home.

Sometime later Jesus cried out, "My God, my God, why have you abandoned me?" The anger of the Holy God against all sin was now about to strike his own Son, who at that moment became sin.[297]In the darkness of that day Jesus experienced the deeper darkness of separation from God his Father.

Isaiah had written. 'It was the Lord's will to crush him and cause him to suffer.'[298]Peter, speaking not long after this dark day said, "This man was handed over to you by God's set purpose and foreknowledge, and you, with the help of wicked men put him to death by nailing him to the cross."[299]

"I'm thirsty," he said. A jar of wine vinegar was there and someone soaked a sponge in it and fixed it to the end of a stem and lifted it to Jesus' lips for him to drink, "It's finished," As Jesus said this, the soldier who was seething with hate for Jesus lost control and taking his spear he plunged it upwards into Jesus' side. Jesus gave out a loud cry and a sudden flow of blood and water came from the deep wound. Before death quickly came, Jesus, in a loud voice, called out, "Father, into your hands I commit my spirit." With those words he bowed his head and died.

The centurion in charge saw the soldier who used his spear on Jesus and was angered by that savage attack; later he dealt with the man as he deserved. Having seen the way Jesus conducted himself and what he had spoken from the cross, the centurion was so moved

---

[297]   2Cor 5:21

[298]   Isa 53:11a

[299]   Acts 2:23

that he praised God and said, "This was an innocent and righteous man." When the vast crowd who came to gloat and mock saw what had happened they were filled with guilt and remorse. The women who had followed Jesus from Galilee and had supported his work stood shocked and heartbroken at a distance watching everything.

The two others who were still alive needed to die soon because the religious authorities didn't want their bodies left on the crosses during what was to be a special Sabbath[300]and so they asked Pilate to order that their legs be broken which he granted. The four soldiers split into two pairs and went first to the crucified men on either side of Jesus and broke their legs which brought death a lot quicker as they soon suffocated, but there was no need to break the legs of Jesus as he was already dead from the lance thrust and his loss of blood.

As part of the instructions Moses was given in regard to the killing and eating of the Passover lamb was that none of its bones were to be broken[301]and the prophet Zechariah was inspired to write, 'They will look on me, the one they have pierced and they will mourn for him as one mourns for an only child and grieve bitterly for him as one grieves for a firstborn son.[302]

A member of the ruling council, named Joseph, who was waiting for the kingdom of God, went to Pilate and asked for the body of Jesus. He had not consented to its decision to kill Jesus, because he was a believer in Jesus, yet secretly. Pilate was surprised to hear that Jesus was already dead and checked with the centurion if it were true, and having been assured that he was dead Pilate gave permission for Joseph to take the body. Nicodemus, who had spoken to Jesus at night, accompanied him. They had about seventy-five pounds of

---

[300]   The first Day of Unleavened Bread which was the first of the seven annual Sabbaths.

[301]   Ex 12:46

[302]   Zec 12:10

myrrh and aloes and they took, with the help of their servants, the body of Jesus down from the darkly stained cross and wrapped it, with the spices, in strips of linen. Close to where Jesus was crucified there was a garden where there was a new tomb that Joseph owned and it had not been used before, and because it was close by and the Sabbath was soon to arrive when they wouldn't be able to continue, they laid him there. The tomb was cut out of rock, and together they rolled a stone against the entrance.

The women had watched the entombment of Jesus and then went home to prepare spices and perfumes but rested on that special annual Sabbath in obedience to the commandment.

Isaiah had written, 'He was oppressed and afflicted yet he did not open his mouth; he was led like a lamb to the slaughter and as a sheep before her shearers is silent so he did not open his mouth. By oppression and judgment he was taken away, and who can speak of his descendants? Because he was cut off from the land of the living; for the transgression of my people he was struck. He was assigned a grave with the wicked and with the rich in his death though he had done no violence nor was there any deceit in his mouth.'[303]

On that Sabbath – the First Day of unleavened Bread – the chief priests and the Pharisees went to see Pilate. Being hypocrites they cared more about ending any possibility of Jesus gaining more disciples after his death than resting on the Sabbath as the women, who were there when he died, were doing.

"We remember," the chief priests and the Pharisees said to Pilate, "that this deceiver said, 'After three days I will rise again.' Because of this, give the order for the tomb to be made secure until the third day, otherwise his disciples might come and steal the body and then

---

[303]   Isa 53:7-9

tell people that he has been raised from the dead and then the last deception will be worse than the first."

"Take a guard," Pilate said to them, "and go, make the tomb as secure as you can." They then went and made the tomb secure by putting a seal on the stone and posting the guard.

The Messiah rises

When the popularity of Jesus was growing and the crowds increasing, Jesus had said to the Pharisees and the teachers of the law, who had told him that they wanted to see a miraculous sign from him, "This is a wicked generation – it asks for a miraculous sign – but none will be given it except the sign of the prophet Jonah, because as Jonah was three days and three nights in the stomach of a huge fish, so the Son of Man will be three days and three nights in the heart of the earth,"[304]

The week that Jesus died had two Sabbaths, the weekly, and the first of the annual Sabbaths. John wrote that the day after he died was a special Sabbath.[305]Jesus was placed in the tomb just as that preparation day was ending at the setting of the sun. Counting three days and three nights would bring us to the time and day of the resurrection and perhaps the best way of finding out exactly when it was is to work backwards, and the accounts we have tell us that when the women came to the tomb on the first day of the week, the sun had not yet risen as it was still dark.

Taking the day before, which was the weekly Sabbath, as one day, and then counting the nights and days until we reach the three days and three nights that Jesus spoke of we come to Wednesday as the day he died and the Tuesday night was when they ate the Passover

---

304   Matt 12:38-40

305   John 19:31

meal. This means that the period of time when he lay dead in the tomb ended Saturday, just before sunset.[306]

The women were the first to see the risen Messiah, and he said to them not to be afraid but to tell the disciples to go to Galilee where they would see him.

As the women hurriedly made their way back into the city the guards were reporting what had happened at the site of the tomb. They spoke of a violent earthquake as a powerful angelic being shining in brilliant light descended from the sky and that he went to the entrance of the tomb and rolled back the heavy stone as if it had no weight, and then sat on it. They told the chief priests that after that they didn't remember what happened because in their fear and shock they all collapsed.

The chief priests believed none of this and thought it was a cover for them having fallen asleep instead of keeping watch, and so to limit any possible damage the missing body of Jesus might generate they gave a large sum of money to the guards to say that while they were asleep his disciples came during the night and stole the body. They assured them that if any of this got back to the governor they would keep them out of trouble. The story that the disciples stole the body of Jesus circulated widely from that time.

The two disciples who had seen and talked with Jesus on the road to Emmaus had returned to Jerusalem and were excitedly telling the eleven, and the others who were with them, everything that had happened, and that they only recognised who he was when he broke the bread, and as they described in detail what he had said Jesus himself stood there and greeted them, "Peace be with you," he said. Fear and shock gripped them and with open mouths and wide eyes they could not believe what they were seeing. The doors had been

---

[306]   Mark 16:9 has, 'When Jesus rose early on the first day of the week,' however; the earliest manuscripts do not have Mark 16:9-20.

locked! "What's troubling you and why can't you believe? Look at my hands and my feet and my side – it's me! Touch me and see – I'm not a ghost; I'm real."

They were so dumfounded and amazed that they still couldn't believe it. "Do you have anything to eat?" Jesus asked them. There was some broiled fish there and so they gave him a piece and with their eyes fastened on him he picked it up and ate it.

"This is what I told you while I was still with you, that everything must be fulfilled that is written about me in the Law of Moses, the Prophets and the Psalms." Then he opened their minds so that they could understand the Scriptures.

This happened on the fourth day of Unleavened Bread. Thomas was not with them and so when he came the others told him that they had seen the Lord, but he did not believe them and said, "Unless I see the nail marks and put my finger where the nails were and put my hand into his side, I will not believe it."

Four days after the Feast had ended they were all together again and Thomas was with them. The doors were locked out of fear of the authorities and Jesus appeared, just as had happened the first time, and he said, "Peace be with you." Looking at Thomas he said, "Put your finger here and look at my hands, and put your hand into my side. Stop doubting and believe."

"My Lord and my God," was all Thomas could say as he fell to his knees.

"Because you've seen me," Jesus said, "you've believed. Blessed are those who haven't seen and yet have believed."

The disciples had returned to Galilee and Peter said that he was going fishing and the others agreed to go with him. Apart from Peter there was Thomas, Nathanael, John, James and two other disciples.

That night of fishing ended without a catch and as the sun was rising a man on the beach called out asking if they had caught anything.

"No, nothing," they called back.

"Throw your net on the right side and you'll find some," the man answered.

When they did they were not able to haul the net in because it was full. John was looking at this stranger on the beach and he turned to Peter and said, "It's the Lord!" As soon as Peter heard that he wrapped his outer garment around him and jumped into the water. John and the others remained in the boat as they towed the net towards the shore.

When they landed they saw a fire of burning coals with fish on it and some bread.

"Bring some of the fish you've just caught," Jesus said to them. Peter helped bring the net ashore and after a count found that the net contained 153 fish and incredibly the net was not broken.

"Come and have breakfast," Jesus invited them, and none of them dared ask him, "Who are you?" as they knew who it was. Jesus took the bread and gave it to them with the fish he had cooked. This was the third time Jesus appeared to his disciples after he was raised from the dead.

After the meal was finished Jesus talked to Peter. Using his full name he said, "Simon son of John, do you truly love me more than these?" Peter remembered saying to Jesus that he would gladly go with him to prison and even to death. He also remembered swearing that he didn't know him.

"Yes Lord, you know that I love you."

"Feed my lambs," Jesus said.

"Simon son of John, do you truly love me?"

"Yes Lord, you know I love you."

"Take care of my sheep."

"Simon son of John, do you love me?"

"Lord, you know all things – you know that I love you." Peter was hurt over the repeated question.

"Feed my sheep. I'm telling you the truth, when you were younger you dressed yourself and went wherever you wanted, but when you're old you'll stretch out your hands and someone else will dress you and lead you where you don't want to go. Follow me"

As they walked Peter looked behind and saw John following them, and he asked Jesus, "Lord, what about John?"

"If I want him to remain alive until I return, what's that to you? You must follow me."

This statement led to a rumour spreading among the disciples that John would not die, but Jesus never said that. He only said, "If I want him to remain alive until I return, what's that to you?"

After Jesus suffered and died he showed himself to his disciples and gave many convincing proofs that he was alive. He appeared to them over a period of forty days and spoke about the kingdom of God. On one occasion, while he was eating with them, he gave them a command not to leave Jerusalem but to wait there for the gift that his Father had promised which he had spoken to them about. "For John," he said to them, "baptised in water but in a few days you will be baptised with the Holy Spirit." Their minds will be connected to the mind of God.

On their last day together, they asked him, "Lord, are you going to restore the kingdom to Israel in our time?"

"It's not for you to know the times or dates the Father has set by his own authority, but you will receive power when the Holy Spirit comes on you, and you will be my witnesses in Jerusalem and in all Judea and Samaria and to the ends of the earth."

They were in the vicinity of Bethany when he said this and then he lifted his hands and blessed them and while he was blessing them he was taken up into the sky and a cloud hid him from view. As they stared intently up into the sky two men dressed in white appeared standing beside them.

"Men of Galilee," one of them said, "why do you stand here looking at the sky?" This same Jesus, who has been taken from you into heaven, will come back in the same way you've seen him go." Then they worshipped him and returned to Jerusalem with great joy and they were continually at the temple praising God.

This was the beginning of the last days.

The Messiah's Spirit

The apostle Paul, who at one time wanted to destroy all followers of Jesus, wrote to the Philippians about Jesus saying that they should be like-minded, having the same love, being one in spirit and purpose, and he went on to say, 'Your attitude should be the same as that of Christ Jesus (or, Let this mind be in you, which was also in Christ Jesus) who, being in nature God, did not consider equality with God something to be grasped, but made himself nothing, taking the very nature of a servant, being made in human likeness, and being found in appearance as a man, he humbled himself and became obedient to death – even death on a cross.

'Because of this God exalted him to the highest place and gave him the name that is above every name, that at the name of Jesus every knee should bow, in heaven and on earth and under the earth, and every tongue confess that Jesus Christ is Lord, to the glory of God the Father.'[307]

Jesus spoke much of the Holy Spirit to his disciples because he was going away, yet they would still need him, and so he had promised that his presence would be with them always, even to the end of the age.

He told them that his presence would be even greater than it had been when he was with them because as a human being he was

---

[307]   Phil 2:2-11

limited to how many people he could be with, but when he returned to his Father his divine nature will then be able to be with all those whom God had called.

"I will come to you," Jesus told them, "I will not leave you as orphans."[308]He will be as one who comes alongside as a helper or defender – a friend at court. As John was later to write, 'If anybody does sin we have one who speaks to the Father in our defence – Jesus Christ, the Righteous One.[309]Paul wrote in the same way, 'Who will bring any charge against those whom God has chosen? It's God who justifies so who is he who condemns? It was Christ Jesus who died and who was raised to life and now is at the right hand of God – where he is also interceding for us.'[310]

His followers will receive the Spirit of truth who will guide them into all truth just as Jesus did when he was with them, "I am the way," Jesus said to Thomas, "and the truth and the life."[311]The truth was what Jesus brought and as we listen to him that truth is implanted in us. Those who do not listen to him do not have the truth.

Paul taught that 'the man without the Spirit does not accept the things that come from the Spirit of God because they are foolish to him and he cannot understand them because they are spiritually discerned.' He goes on to say, 'we have the mind of Christ.' And he later wrote, 'and I think that I too have the Spirit of God.'[312]Remember what Paul said to the Philippians, 'Your attitude (or your mind) should be the same as Christ Jesus.' Having the mind of Christ is the same as having the Spirit of God.[313]The two expressions mean the same thing.

---

308   John 14:!8

309   1 John 2:1

310   Rom 8:33-34

311   John 14:6

312   1Cor 7:40b

313   1 Cor 2:16, 7:40

David wrote, 'Where can I go from your Spirit? Where can I flee from your presence?'[314] God's presence, his mind, and his Spirit, are one and the same thing. Our spirit is our character and attitude, as David, in an earlier psalm, prayed for 'a steadfast spirit and a willing spirit,' he is speaking of his mind and attitude, just as having the mind of Christ is another way of saying having the Spirit of God.

Jesus said, in the context of receiving another Counsellor, "If anyone loves me, he will obey my teaching. My Father will love him and we will come to him and make our home with him."[315] Then Jesus said, "But the Counsellor, the Holy Spirit, whom the father will send in my name will teach you all things and will remind you of everything I have said to you." The reality of what he said being later accurately written down, and that we are able to read those words so long after he spoke them, is the fulfilment of his promise.

"You have one teacher," Jesus told the religious authorities, "the Messiah."[316] The Holy Spirit as our teacher, and Jesus as our teacher, does not make two teachers as there is only one. There is one Spirit, and one teacher. While Jesus was here he taught within the limitations of being one person, but from heaven his Spirit, or mind, is poured out on all believers. Peter describes it as 'participating in the divine nature.'[317]

The Spirit of God is the Spirit of Christ which means that God lives in us and that we belong to Christ.[318] There is one Spirit, one God the Father, and one Lord. Peter writes that the prophets in the Old Testament wrote of Christ by the Spirit of Christ that was in them

---

314   Psa 139:7

315   John 14:23

316   Matt 23:10

317   2 Peter 1:4

318   Rom 8:9

who was then spoken of as the Lord, as in, 'The word of the Lord came to me."[319]

Isaiah calls him, 'Wonderful Counsellor, Mighty God, Everlasting Father, Prince of peace.' This is in the same section as, 'For to us a child is born, to us a son is given and the government will be on his shoulders and he will be called...'[320]

Our spirit is our character, which returns to God when we die – there it 'rests' or 'sleeps' until awakened from that sleep at the resurrection, and then united with an indestructible spiritual body which joins with Christ, and all the other resurrected saints, in restoring all things – the establishment of God's kingdom here on earth.

That Counsellor which Jesus sends not only lives in the Christian and intercedes for them, he also exposes the guilt of the world. Just as Jesus did against sin in his generation and so he will do that same exposing of sin through his people in all the generations that are to follow. "Shout it aloud," Isaiah writes, "don't hold back – raise your voice like a trumpet. Declare to my people their rebellion and to the house of Jacob their sins.'[321] Yet not only does the world reject what Jesus says but many who claim to represent him speak only of the pleasant and comfortable things that relate to God and refuse to confront people with the real Jesus who spoke of sin, judgment and righteousness. Because of the extent of the dragon's deception when sin and judgment is addressed many are misdirected away from what Jesus taught to the lie of the wicked being tormented for an eternity and away from the needs of this world to the saved leaving it to spend an eternity in heaven.

---

[319]   1 Peter 1:10-11, Jer 1:4

[320]   Isa 9:6

[321]   Isa 58:1. See Isaiah 30:8-11.

'No-one knows the thoughts of God except the Spirit of God. We have not received the spirit of the world but the Spirit who is from God, that we may understand what God has freely given us.'[322]When Jesus sat by the well talking to the Samaritan woman he said to her, "A time is coming, and has now come when the true worshippers will worship the Father in spirit and in truth because they are the kind of worshippers the Father seeks. God is spirit and his worshippers must worship in spirit and in truth."[323]

GOD IS SPIRIT, different from us; we have a spirit in us – a part of us that is non-physical which enables us to reason, to contemplate and obey, or disobey. It is our character and nature. However, at its core it is sinful and alienated from God, unless the Father enables us to come to Christ.[324]But God does not have a spirit as we do –he is spirit – and he is holy – and so he is the Holy Spirit, and all the promises relating to the Holy Spirit are speaking of God himself, not of another person. In the symbolic language of Revelation images are given of God's throne in heaven and the Lamb, who also sits on a throne, apart from them there are multitudes of angels but no other divine person, except the twenty-four elders and the four living creatures.[325]There is no third divine person – that misleading teaching came much later and people were forced by law to accept it, even though many opposed it then and later.

William Barclay in his book, 'The plain man looks at the Apostles' creed' writes on the subject of the Trinity; 'It is important and helpful to remember that the word Trinity is not itself a New Testament word. It is even true at least in one sense to say that the doctrine of the Trinity is not directly a New Testament doctrine. It is rather a deduction from, and an interpretation of, the thought and language

---

[322]   1Cor 1:11-12

[323]   John 4:23-24

[324]   John 6:44,65

[325]   Rev 5

of the New Testament. The most important fact of all to remember is that it was not a doctrine which anyone in the Church ever sat down and, as it were, worked out from first principles by a series of logical steps; the doctrine of the Trinity has been from the beginning, and must always be seen as, an interpretation of actual Christian experience.'[326]

Salvation is a rescue mission accomplished on an enemy held planet. We who escape death, slavery and wrath do not need or require humanly devised creeds when Scripture is fully adequate for informing us of what salvation is. The apostle Paul does this very effectively in a section that John Stott said is 'a condensed but comprehensive account of salvation.'[327]

'At one time we too were foolish, disobedient, deceived and enslaved by all kinds of passions and pleasures. We lived in malice and envy, being hated and hating one another. But when the kindness and love of God our Saviour appeared, he saved us, not because of righteous things we had done, but because of his mercy. He saved us through the washing of rebirth and renewal by the Holy Spirit, whom he poured out on us generously through Jesus Christ our Saviour, so that, having been justified by his grace, we might become heirs having the hope of eternal life.'[328]

The spirit who speaks to the seven churches of revelation is Christ.[329]He speaks to us today in just the same way as when Joshua was commissioned to take over after Moses, Christ said to him, "Be strong and courageous. Do not be terrified; do not be discouraged

---

[326]   To find out how, and when, and by whom the teaching of the Trinity came to be a foundational teaching of the church see my book, 'The Dragon the World and the Christian' page 89.

[327]   The Message of 1 Timothy & Titus, page 201.

[328]   Titus 3:3-7

[329]   Rev 2:7, 11, 17, 26-29, 3:6,11-13,19-22.

because the Lord your God will be with you wherever you go."[330] The people of Israel were also told to be strong and courageous, "Do not be afraid or terrified because of them (the Canaanites) for the Lord your God goes with you; he will never leave you nor forsake you."[331] But they were rebellious and stubborn and refused to obey God and so eventually they lost everything. We too can lose everything if we refuse to listen to him – he is the word of God and his words can cut deep in exposing our attitudes and motives.

Jesus came as the righteous and obedient Israelite and did what they, the ancient Israelites, and we, failed to do. He now calls people from all races to be the true Israel – the people of God – called out of this world to become like him. He leaves behind not only his promise 'never to leave or forsake you,' but his Spirit – his very mind and nature – so that we can, in part, see as he sees, and grow towards thinking as he thinks, until that day when he appears and our sinful nature, which so easily entangles us, will no longer be a part of us. Then, at the resurrection, we will be like him and we will see him as he is. Until then we wait in the sleep of death, or are changed instantly, if we are alive at his return.

John wrote in one of his letters, 'That which was from the beginning, which we have heard, which we have seen with our eyes, which we have looked at and our hands have touched – this is what we proclaim concerning the Word of life. The life appeared – we have seen it and we proclaim to you the eternal life, which was with the Father and has appeared to us. We proclaim what we have seen and heard so that you may have fellowship with us, and our fellowship is with the Father and with his Son, Jesus the Messiah.[332]

The bitter conflicts that we see in our own communities and the violence, injustice and cruelty which is daily in our newspapers and

---

[330]   Jos 1:9

[331]   Deut 31:6

[332]   1 John 1:1-3

on our screens provide the undeniable evidence of the deep divisions that exist between humans. Sectarianism within Christianity is also evidence of the very real differences that also exists within a body of people who should be the ones who exhibit the love, goodwill and submission to a heavenly Father just as the author of their liberation did. The distinctive differences of tradition and teaching reflect a disunity that more resembles the society we live in rather than as representatives of the Kingdom of God. This religious confusion will not continue indefinitely. Its fractures will not be healed by any individual or combination of churches working together, neither will revolution or reformation bring peace on earth.

The churches' divisions, along with the world's conflicts, will continue and worsen until the good news that Jesus brought becomes a reality. That earth changing event is the overthrow of all human government and the establishment of a divine alien government led by the one that the world rejected, and still does. God's people are not divided, and they are one – their number known only to him – even though they are scattered among very different fellowships and even outside of any. They are the chosen and elected ones who constitute the body of Christ. They have the mind of the Messiah and belong to him. His people pray and wait for that day, because it is humanly impossible to solve the problems that our own nature creates. Coupled with our sinful nature is the unseen spiritual ruler of this world who has conned all of us in different ways. That evil entity will be removed so that he can no longer deceive us. At that time we will all see what is true, and what is counterfeit. The true light will return to eradicate all darkness.

The Anointed One – Christ – the Messiah, will return and real peace will come at last as his rule encircles the earth. That is the good news. This dark age ends and the age of light begins.

He promises to come soon and his people respond; "Yes, come Lord Jesus – your Kingdom come!"

Last thoughts

James knew that this was the day he would die. He had been arrested along with other followers of the Messiah on the orders of Herod. As he was lead to his execution he remembered standing next to his brother, John, as they both confidently asserted that they were ready to drink from the same cup that Jesus was about to drink from and experience suffering and death as his disciples.

Through their mother, Jesus and the other disciples learned of their personal ambition to sit at the right hand and the left hand of Jesus when he rules over his kingdom. Both James and John were known for being aggressive and had once wanted to obliterate a Samaritan village that did not welcome Jesus because he was heading for Jerusalem. Jesus reprimanded them for their violent attitude. They needed to learn that being a servant of the Messiah was the highest position a person could receive and to learn to love their enemies rather than kill them which came a lot more naturally.

In those last moments before James reached the spot where the swordsman waited he thought back to something Jesus said to them at that last Passover meal.

"You are my friends if you do what I command. I no longer call you servants, because a servant doesn't know his master's business. Instead, I have called you friends, because everything that I learned from my Father I have made known to you. You didn't choose me, but I chose you and appointed you to go and bear fruit – fruit that will last. Then my Father will give you whatever you ask in my name. This is my command. Love each other."

'You are my friends.' With that thought he knelt down. The sword was swung and sunlight flashed from the blade as the head of James was separated from his body.

His brother lived a long life, mostly in Ephesus. Mary, the mother of Jesus, lived there with him. During the reign of Domitian John was exiled to the rocky island of Patmos but when Domitian died those he had sent into exile were released. John then wrote the book of Revelation addressed to the seven churches in western Turkey.

Polycarp was taught by John and Polycrates used his example of observing the Passover on a fixed date of the month rather than a fixed day of the week (Sunday). In a letter he sent to Victor, who was bishop of Rome, he wrote, 'I am not scared of threats.' This was when Victor had threatened in AD 190 to excommunicate those who celebrated the Last Supper according to the Hebrew calendar. When the churches in the east refused to get in line with Rome Victor excommunicated them. Polycrates, who was bishop of Ephesus, was not intimidated into giving in to Victor's threats and continued in the tradition that had come down from John.

Rome's dominance finally won the argument at the Council of Nicaea in AD 325. By that time the word Passover had ceased to be used and had been replaced by the name of Easter; a word with pagan origins. These and other disputes were to continue down the centuries and the history of Christianity is stained with the blood of those who dared to disagree with the church authorities. 'Choice was threatening to Christian thinkers, who saw religious unity – even coerced religious unity – as the only alternative to chaos.'[333]

---

[333]   Alan Kreider in the foreword to Meic Pearse's 'The Great Restoration – The Religious Radicals of the 16th and 17th Centuries.'

None of this was known to James whose execution ended his consciousness.

"James, wake up!" Like the blast of a trumpet a powerful voice caused James to open his eyes. He was no longer in the kneeling position of his last memory but standing in a street unlike any street he had known and it was dark but not the darkness of night. Looking around he saw many desperate and frightened people who were running in different directions, most of whom were searching for a place to hide. Some were wearing armour that he did not recognise and carried equipment that was strange to him. Huge iron machines moved passed him making a deafening noise and filling the air with smoke. Tall damaged buildings that surrounded him were unrecognisable from the Jerusalem he had known.

"The master is returning and I've come to escort you to him." James turned to see a man dressed in gleaming white standing next to him. "Hold my hand," the stranger said and James took his hand and looked at the man's face who smiled back at him and James knew that this servant of God was one of the angels that Jesus had promised to send at his return to gather his people to meet him.

"Are you ready?" asked the angel. James nodded and to the shock of those around them they flew up into the dark and reddish sky. Both he and the angel were fast moving points lights that drew a bright line as they left the earth's atmosphere. He looked around him and saw other couplings soaring upwards, and further away more narrow beams of lights were curving over the horizon heading in their direction. Very soon these individual figures became a wide and powerful force of united light surging into the darkness of space.

James tilted his head back as they raced upwards and he saw an even greater brilliance coming down to meet them. His eyes scanned what looked like millions of angels and at its centre he looked into the light that no human eye could look at and saw his master and friend. Both forces of light began to merge and for a moment pause in space then this incredibly bright mass of light turned towards earth.

Their descent was seen on earth to be aimed at a region very close to Jerusalem. In spite of worldwide disasters on a scale never seen before most of humanity cursed the name of God and neither repented or glorified him. To the military forces that were gathered in Israel to fight each other their combined forces now, because of their fear at what was fast approaching them, turned their weapons at what appeared to be an alien invasion, but the splendour of this divine light was also a destructive energy that no human could survive when they came into contact with it.

God had told Moses that no-one could see him and live, and now God's enemies were about to encounter that presence. It was over very quickly. They were all dead even before what was left of them hit the ground. The divine army landed on the Mount of Olives, just as the angels had told the disciples when Jesus had left them and the impact of their arrival was so great that it caused an earthquake. The mount was split in two from east to west which formed a great valley and with half the mount moving north and half moving south, just as the prophet Zechariah had said would happen on that day.

James saw some that he recognised and many others he did not, but they were all now immortal and powerful. With unspeakable joy they all knew that they were now without any of their previous sinful nature and were qualified to rule with their king and use their wisdom and power to restore God's government across the world.

James listened as the King spoke to him, at the same time he also spoke to all the others. They all heard as individuals and knew what was to happen next.

Their work was about to begin.

There was much to do.

The kingdoms of the world were now the kingdom of the Messiah.

About the Author

Phil Hinsley was born in Barry, South Wales. He studied graphic art in Cardiff and moved to London to pursue a career in photography. Later he turned to portrait painting and exhibited at the Royal Academy, the Royal Society of Portrait Painters and the National Portrait Gallery. He worked for 25 years at Leavesden hospital, a place for people with learning difficulties where he had a year out as their artist in residence. His murals were shortlisted for the Astra Arts competition in 1991.

He now works for the site team of Watford Grammar School for Girls. He is married to Anne and they occasionally have gerbils.

From 1968 he was a member of the Worldwide Church of God, and when they had a radical reordering of their teachings in 1993-4 he fully supported those changes and was later active in lay preaching and in the church's evangelistic programme. However, he had serious questions over the type of evangelism he was required to do, believing that sin, God's law and repentance needed to be addressed and finding, to his growing frustrating, that to point to our need for repentance was not allowed, rather, people were asked if there was anything they were going through that the church could pray about. This, to his mind, was neglecting their greatest need – to be right with God. This softer approach to evangelism struck him as only dealing with secondary issues and he strongly believed that it was not in line with the way that was consistent with what Jesus did – to be confrontational – to speak of sin, righteousness and judgment. Because of this frustration he left their fellowship and began looking for a church that had a more biblical approach to evangelism.

After a few months he found it in a small local church which had been newly planted by a Grace Baptist pastor. Joining them he was soon involved with street ministry and going from door to door, but over a period of time he realised that he was not in agreement with some of their core teachings, which are shared by the majority of Christian denominations. He wrote and circulated to the leadership some papers on those points of disagreement, but he found himself being warned against sharing his thoughts. He then reluctantly decided to resign from the fellowship rather than become a backseat critic, and possibly sowing discord amongst the congregation.

It was not just that he found the theology of two fellowships unbiblical, but that he came to realise that all of us, whether with faith or having none, have been conned. The scale of this deception is staggering. He came to believe that, as Scripture says, Satan has led the whole world astray. This, he saw, was why the churches are divided and fractured into thousands of fellowships, some of which thinking that they are the only ones that are right and all the others are wrong, but it is so easy to see the mistakes of others while failing to recognise our own. He recognised this attitude because he used to take the same position. This is the reason he turned to writing. He is not against any church or individuals but wants to identify how and why, and by whom, all of us, without exception, have been taken in on some of the most foundational teachings of Christianity.

There are Christians who do not believe that Satan as an individual being exists or that his number one intention is to destroy God's people – his secondary intention is to mislead and deceive them – but this unbiblical view that all evil is generated by man alone is not what Jesus and the New Testament writers taught. If we can acknowledging that Satan has led astray all of us, which is a big step, and in particular, the Christian church, an even bigger step, then the four most commonly accepted beliefs that millions understand as true need to be re-examined. They are; the eternal suffering of the lost in hell, the immortality of our souls, that the saved will go to heaven, and lastly, the most important teaching for the majority of Christians; the Trinity.

These four doctrinal teachings have been grafted into traditional teaching, yet, through correlating all the verses from both testaments on each of these four important teachings the open-minded and objective Bible student can only conclude that these essential teachings have come from another source than the Bible. Although a strong argument can be made for this unorthodox position the majority of people will not accept it unless a number of highly placed individuals, who are respected church leaders, make this paradigm change first.

Even though it is highly unlikely that traditionally held beliefs will be jettisoned he believes that we do need to be alerted to these highly misleading teachings and the distorting of biblical texts over the reality of heaven, hell, our souls and the Holy Spirit, as well as the future of earth.

He no longer attends any fellowship but believes in the unity of God's one church scattered throughout the denominations and even outside of them. There is not one fellowship that has not, in one way or another, been deceived on some major point of teaching and so by taking himself away from regular attendance he can more freely speak and write on these important issues. He looks forward and prays for the return of the Messiah to bring an end to Satan's hold on the world and to the establishment of God's kingdom here on earth.

9907713R00143

Printed in Great Britain
by Amazon.co.uk, Ltd.,
Marston Gate.